RAIN CHECK

ADMIT ONE - Subject to the conditions set forth on the back hereof.

SECOND RAIN CHECK in the event of a postponement this coupon will admit the holder to the game numbered hereon. Not good if detached from Original Rain Check.

"BASEBALL GIVES EVERY AMERICAN BOY A CHANCE TO EXCEL.
NOT JUST TO BE AS GOOD AS SOMEONE ELSE, BUT TO BE BETTER.
THIS IS THE NATURE OF MAN AND THE NAME OF THE GAME."

★

TED WILLIAMS

ALL CENTURY
★ Team ★

EDITED BY MARK VANCIL & PETER HIRDT ★ PUBLISHED BY RARE AIR BOOKS

TABLE OF CONTENTS

DESIGNED AND PRODUCED BY

RARE AIR MEDIA
1711 North Paulina, Suite 311, Chicago, Illinois 60622

TEXT BY

Written and edited by Mark Vancil and Peter Hirdt
Copyright © 1999 by Rare Air Media
Research and statistical information provided by Elias Sports Bureau, Inc.
Produced in partnership with and licensed by Major League Baseball Properties, Inc.

The authors have attempted to properly credit all sources for historical quotations included in the first
80 pages of the book. As this edition of the *All Century Team* went to press, permissions for all archival
or historical quotes were in process. All permissions will appear in all future editions of the book.

Rare Air books may be purchased for educational, business, or sales promotional use. For information please contact, Jim Forni at Rare Air Media (773) 342-5180.

First Edition
Library of Congress Cataloging-in-Publication Data is available from the Publisher.
ISBN 0-06-107539-6
Printed in the United States of America.
99 00 01 02 RA 10 9 8 7 6 5 4 3 2 1

PHOTOGRAPHY CREDITS

COVER: HANK AARON, WILLIE MAYS, NOLAN RYAN, CAL RIPKEN JR., KEN GRIFFEY JR., YOGI BERRA, PETE ROSE, ERNIE BANKS, JOHNNY BENCH, STAN MUSIAL – **WALTER IOOSS JR.** • ROGERS HORNSBY, WALTER JOHNSON, TY COBB, BROOKS ROBINSON, CHRISTY MATHEWSON, LEFTY GROVE, HONUS WAGNER, JACKIE ROBINSON – **CORBIS** • CY YOUNG, TED WILLIAMS – **MLB PHOTOS** • JOE DIMAGGIO, WARREN SPAHN – **AP/WORLDWIDE** • MICKEY MANTLE – **JOHN ZIMMERMAN** • MIKE SCHMIDT – **RICH PILLING** • ROGER CLEMENS – **HEINZ KLUETMEIER** • MARK MCGWIRE – **V.J. LOVERO** • BABE RUTH – **ARCHIVE PHOTOS** • LOU GEHRIG – **GEORGE BRACE COLLECTION** • BOB GIBSON – **JAMES DRAKE** • SANDY KOUFAX – **NATIONAL BASEBALL LIBRARY COOPERSTOWN, N.Y.**

AP WORLDWIDE PHOTOS	014, 028-029, 048, 055, 068-069, 198	MARC KAUFFMAN, *Sports Illustrated*	045, 080, 081, 096-097, 123, 186-187, 198
ARCHIVE PHOTOS	148-149	HIENZ KLUETMEIER, *Sports Illustrated*	049, 080, 159, 171
ROBERT BECK, *National Baseball Library Cooperstown, N.Y.*	050	LOS ANGELES DODGERS, INC	186
JOHN BIEVER, *Sports Illustrated*	033	NATIONAL BASEBALL LIBRARY COOPERSTOWN, N.Y.	016, 060, 150
GEORGE BRACE COLLECTION	036, 037, 067. 080, 081, 095, 109, 138	KEN LIEBERMAN, *Sports Illustrated*	130
JEFF CARLICK, *National Baseball Library Cooperstown, N.Y.*	045, 051	NEIL LIEFFER, *Sports Illustrated*	045, 141, 147, 188
CORBIS/BETTMAN	014, 023, 024, 033, 040, 053, 063, 067, 067, 072-073, 080, 081, 091, 102-103, 104, 105, 108, 110-111, 118-119, 120-121, 122, 124-25, 128, 132, 133, 134, 135, 136-137, 138, 139, 144, 145, 153, 154-155, 158, 167, 176, 182, 183, 184, 185, 188, 189, 190, 191, 192, 193, 194-195, 196-197, 202, 203, 204-205	V.J. LOVERO, *Sports Illustrated*	080, 081, 113
		JOHN MCDONOUGH	026-027
		JOHN MILLAN	064
		RONALD MODRA, *Sports Illustrated*	013, 156, 213
		MARVIN E. NEWMAN, *Sports Illustrated*	201
		HY PESKIN, *Sports Illustrated*	041, 080, 081, 145, 155, 160-161, 162
		RICH PILLING, *Major League Baseball Photos*	017, 036, 080, 081, 114, 180, 212-213
CULVER PICTURES	149	SPORTSCHROME	013, 025, 065, 158
AURTHER DALEY, *Sports Illustrated*	080, 081, 088, 162	SPORTS IMAGERY	013, 025, 033, 065, 080, 081, 101, 146, 208, 209, 210-211
DAN DONOVAN, *National Baseball Library Cooperstown, N.Y.*	065		
JAMES DRAKE, *Sports Illustrated*	057, 080, 081, 084, 159, 163, 177	HERB SCHARFMAN, *Sports Illustrated*	057
DAVID DUROCHIK, *SportPics*	013, 025, 062, 076, 077, 080, 081, 099, 100, 101, 173	BILL STOVER, *National Baseball Library Cooperstown, N.Y.*	115
		LOUIS DELUCA, *National Baseball Library Cooperstown, N.Y.*	078, 178, 181
JOHN IACONO, *Sports Illustrated*	045, 079, 080, 081, 084, 170	SPORTS ILLUSTRATED	067
INSTITUTE OF TEXAN CULTURES, *San Antonio, Texas*	036	DAMIAN STROHMEYER	078
WALTER IOOSS JR., *Sports Illustrated*	015, 016, 017, 018-019, 023, 030, 031, 032, 033, 034-035, 038-039, 042-043, 045, 046, 047, 053, 054-055, 056-057, 060-061, 064-065, 067, 070-071, 074, 076-077, 080, 081, 086-087, 088, 089, 090, 094, 097, 098-099, 115, 129, 131, 140-141, 142, 143, 144, 145, 157, 162, 167, 172, 174-175, 179, 200, 214-115, 216	TRANSCENDENTAL GRAPHICS	149
		TONY TRIOLO, *Sports Illustrated*	053, 057, 087
		RON VESELY	020-021, 023, 025, 053, 065, 075, 112, 114, 180, 181
		JOHN ZIMMERMAN, *Sports Illustrated*	041, 080, 081, 152,-153, 161, 164, 165

DEDICATION

For my Laurita, Alexandra and Samantha, whose spirit graced this
world during the creation of this book. Their beauty, warmth
and capacity to love is more than any one man deserves. I am blessed beyond
any reasonable expectation for their presence in my life. ★ **MV** 1999

THANK YOU

As long days turn into weeks and the weeks into nearly two months, surface gloss is stripped away and all that's left is the true measure of those with whom you have gone to battle. In publishing terms, particularly given the level at which the *All Century Team* was executed, dozens of individuals worked once more to transform the impossible into the routine. For these contributions, both of spirit and sweat, I worry only that I cannot find the appropriate words or phrases to express the depth of my thanks. So many did so much in such a remarkably short amount of time that I suspect only we ever will know all of what was accomplished. ★ At Major League Baseball, Don Hintze provided us the latitude to execute our vision while driving the program, internally and externally, throughout the process. His staff, particularly Rich Pilling and Paul Cunningham reacted at a moment's notice regardless of the request; Bill Henneberry proved to be a man whose genius extends well beyond the ability to define and connect people and concepts. His is the kind of innate goodness that comes only from an "old soul"; From Chris Brande in videos, Jeremy Cohen in premiums, Rick Platt in retail, Alex Kam in new media and Robyn Frank, baseball backed up a remarkable promotion with back-end execution and assistance; meanwhile, Kathy Francis showed us why the All Century Team program worked so well for so many. She found time amid the chaos to listen to our ideas and provide direction for even the most aggressive among them. ★ All of which came about thanks to the Marketing Centre's Jeff Gehl, whose positive approach and moment to moment drive becomes only more impressive with each day you spend around him. ★ At MasterCard, Jeff Price, Bob Cramer and Tracey Stevens showed us all how to drive a major national program with class and clarity. They listened to our ideas, helped us define the best of them and provided a guiding hand at the point of execution. ★ The opportunity to reconnect with the amazing talents of my friends and former colleagues in the sports writing community reminded me again that journalists possess talents often not fully appreciated by even those for whom they work. Despite full-time jobs and seven children between them, Bob Nightengale of *Baseball Weekly* and Tom Keegan of the *New York Post* never once turned away a request. Still, I remain most grateful for their friendship. ★ To all those who have made Rare Air Media the company it is and the company it is fast becoming, your hard work and commitment to excellence is humbling. John Vieceli and his design staff, including Shereen Boury, Seth Guge, Mark Alper and Steve Polacek, never once strayed from the integrity of their art despite more than 50 straight days that started one morning and ended the next. John's ability to combine leading-edge design with "old school" work ethic and discipline continues to amaze all around him. Jim Forni and his staff, including Carol Scatorchio in New York and Melinda Fry, Heidi Knack and Elizabeth Fulton in Chicago, executed the details with efficiency, class and aplomb despite my usual litany of unreasonable demands and expectations. Meanwhile, Paul Sheridan, Andy Pipitone, Lisa Butler, Jim Carlton, Kyle Worthington and Dennis Carlson continued to drive the company toward the future. ★ Finally, Peter Hirdt and the Elias Sports Bureau proved once more what everyone in the sports world already knows — they play in a league of one. In less than 30 days, Peter turned around more than 30,000 words with a depth of analysis and clarity beyond even our most optimistic expectations. His passion, work ethic and character became obvious to all those with whom he worked at Rare Air. ★ The very nature of shrinking a six-month process into a 45-day window suggests still others whose professionalism and commitment translated into significant contributions:

At The Marketing Centre
Missy Gehl, Brad Barlow
and Courtney Bertasi

At Sports Illustrated
Karen Carpenter and Prem Kalliat

At Professional Graphics
Pat Goley, Steve Goley, David Goley,
Vince Llamzon, Marty Cox

At ACME Printing
Fran Canzano, Lou Berceli
and Susan Schmidt

At Mead Paper
Molly Foshay

At Baseball Hall of Fame
Jim Gates, Bill Burdick

At Corbis
Kevin Rettig

SportPics
Dave Durochik

Special Thanks
Paul Sheridan, Walter Iooss Jr.

*"THERE ARE FIVE THINGS YOU CAN DO IN BASEBALL —
RUN, THROW, CATCH, HIT AND HIT WITH POWER."*

★

LEO DUROCHER, FORMER DODGERS, GIANTS,
CUBS AND ASTROS MANAGER

★ TOOLS ★

Tools. One of the most common words in the common baseball process of advancing and eliminating the dreams of young men. It's on the basis of measuring the quality of five specific abilities — Tools — against the major league norm that young men summarily are separated from the chance of earning a living as a professional ballplayer. For all the grace and goodness that is the game of baseball, the first cut is the deepest by design. Even more cold and calculating than a Bob Gibson fastball or Ty Cobb's spikes-first slides, the dissection of an 18-year-old athlete starts and ends with the eyes of a scout. Tools, they will tell you, predict the future in a way no radar gun or high school batting average ever can. There are other elements that the old timers measure against the tools, subtle messages found in the size of a boy's parents or the way in which a young man carries himself. But these are pinpricks compared to the surgical procedure demanded by a review of a boy's future ability against the reality of his tools today.

"Sometimes you get carried away with somebody," says Spider Jorgensen, a Chicago Cubs scout. "You know some kid. You know the father. You know the mother. Gordon Goldsberry, the legendary scout, always said, 'Look at the tools. See if the guy can run, throw, hit, hit for power. Does he have the glove? You start looking at the tools and then you come back to reality. You don't start dreaming. If the tools are there, he has a chance — especially if he can run and hit.' Gordon used to write me little notes along the way and remind me: 'Look at the tools.'"

To be sure, true greatness extends beyond even the most apparent physical gifts. The sixth tool, though generally measured only after the first five have been decided, is the most mercurial. Intangibles, as they often are described, are those traits consistent with the elite in virtually any athletic endeavor and they have a specific application in baseball. In a game in which 70 percent failure is the mark of a very good hitter, internal characteristics and traits often determine as much as pure physical ability.

"There are guys who have had great tools, guys with great power or great speed, but they couldn't

comprehend what the hell it takes to put those capabilities to use," says Hall of Famer Ralph Kiner. "That's what makes someone special. Figuring out how to put that God-given talent to use."

If the tools eliminate pretenders, then the intangibles separate contenders. Hank Aaron complained after hitting .280 with 13 home runs and 69 RBI that he was embarrassed by his performance. It was his rookie season. Roberto Clemente's "style" was predicated on an innate confidence that fueled almost constant aggression. Joe DiMaggio played with bone spurs so bad that he often tiptoed through the clubhouse after games late in his career. Lefty Grove, who walked as many batters as he struck out for years, once struck out Babe Ruth, Lou Gehrig and Tony Lazzeri on nine pitches with a runner on third base. Aaron, Barry Bonds, Ken Griffey Jr., Greg Maddux, Whitey Ford and Ted Williams, to name only a few, dissected opponents on the sidelines long before they ever attacked the found weakness on the field.

"At this level, there's not a huge difference in talent," says Baltimore's B.J. Surhoff, a member of the 1999 American League All-Star team. "Players who are above the rest are the ones who are there day after day. They are willing to accomplish something great every day and they are not afraid to fail. They are there day after day, year after year. There are a lot of talented players who can't do that, who can't be there day after day because they don't understand the nature of that kind of approach. That's what separates the good ones from the great ones."

Of the more than 15,000 players who put on a Major League uniform in the 20th Century only 100 were deemed worthy of the All Century Team. What divided those players from one another is what always has divided the big leagues from the minor leagues and the minor leagues from the sandlot: Tools. But at the level of the 100, and the dozen or so heading into that class in the 21st Century, the differences are far more subtle than the speed on a fastball or the ability to line a hard slider to the opposite field. For them, excellence is a matter of degree, true greatness a consequence of place, time, opportunity and circumstance.

In other words, the cream always rises.

"YOU HAVE A 100 MORE YOUNG KIDS THAN YOU HAVE A PLACE FOR ON YOUR CLUB. EVERY ONE OF 'EM HAS HAD A GOIN' AWAY PARTY. THEY HAVE BEEN GIVEN THE SHAVING KIT AND THE $50. THEY KISSED EVERYBODY AND SAID, 'SEE YOU IN THE MAJORS IN TWO YEARS.' YOU SEE THESE POOR KIDS WHO SHOULDN'T EVEN BE THERE IN THE FIRST PLACE. YOU WRITE ON THE REPORT CARD '4-4-4 AND OUT.' THAT'S THE LOWEST RATING IN EVERYTHING. THEN YOU CALL 'EM IN AND SAY, 'IT'S THE CONSENSUS AMONG US THAT WE'RE GOING TO LET YOU GO BACK HOME.' SOME OF 'EM CRY. SOME GET MAD. BUT NONE OF 'EM WILL LEAVE UNTIL YOU ANSWER 'EM ONE QUESTION: 'SKIPPER, WHAT DO YOU THINK?' AND YOU HAVE TO LOOK EVERY ONE OF THOSE KIDS IN THE EYE AND KICK THEIR DREAMS IN THE BUTT AND SAY NO. IF YOU SAY IT MEAN ENOUGH, MAYBE THEY DO THEMSELVES A FAVOR AND DON'T WASTE YEARS LEARNING WHAT YOU CAN SEE IN A DAY. THEY DON'T HAVE WHAT IT TAKES TO MAKE THE MAJORS. JUST LIKE I NEVER HAD IT."

★

EARL WEAVER TO TOM BOSWELL IN THE *Washington Post*

"I was sitting in an airport with Calvin Griffith in Toronto the year the All-Star Game was there, asking him about players he saw that I never got a chance to see, guys like Walter Johnson and Ty Cobb. He was 18 when Ty Cobb came in and asked him to throw batting practice to him. Before hitting, Cobb would take 3x5 pieces of paper and put them in the outfield in places that absolutely would be a base hit if the ball landed there. Then he would practice hitting line drives to hit those pieces of paper. When he told me that I got so excited my heart started beating fast. It all goes back to that specific pregame preparation. The common thread for greatness is doing those things necessary to achieve your goals that you don't necessarily like to do all the time."

★

SYD THRIFT, ASSISTANT GENERAL MANAGER OF THE BALTIMORE ORIOLES,
AUTHOR, INNOVATIVE BASEBALL EXECUTIVE AND INSTRUCTOR

"AS FAR AS I'M CONCERNED, AARON IS THE BEST BALLPLAYER OF MY ERA. ...HE IS TO BASEBALL OF THE LAST 15 YEARS WHAT JOE DIMAGGIO WAS BEFORE HIM. HE HAS NEVER RECEIVED THE CREDIT HE'S DUE. I STILL THINK THE AMERICAN LEAGUE IS BETTER BUT THE NATIONAL LEAGUE HAS MORE OUTSTANDING STARS. THE BEST ONE IS HANK AARON. TED WILLIAMS IS THE BEST HITTER I EVER SAW BUT DIMAGGIO WAS THE MOST FINISHED PLAYER. JOE COULD HIT, THROW, FIELD AND RUN THE BASES. I PUT AARON IN THE SAME CATEGORY. HE IS LOOSE AND AGILE AS A CAT. WHEN HE HITS THE BALL — MAN, IT'S LIKE THUNDER. AND HE NEVER MAKES A MISTAKE."

★ MICKEY MANTLE, 1969

400/400

OF SPEED AND POWER, CONSIDER THAT ONLY THREE PLAYERS WITH AS MANY STOLEN BASES HIT HALF AS MANY HOME RUNS (RICKY HENDERSON, JOE MORGAN AND PAUL MOLITOR) AND NONE OF THEM IS WITHIN 150 HOME RUNS OF BONDS. AT THE SAME TIME, OF THE 22 PLAYERS WITH AS MANY HOME RUNS AS BONDS, ONLY TWO STOLE HALF AS MANY BASES (WILLIE MAYS AND HANK AARON) AND NEITHER IS WITHIN 100 STEALS OF BONDS.

IT'S ONLY FITTING THAT BARRY BONDS WOULD BE ON PACE TO BECOME THE ONLY PLAYER IN HISTORY TO STEAL 400 BASES AND HIT 400 HOME RUNS. HIS FATHER, BOBBY BONDS, IS THE ONLY PLAYER TO HAVE MULTIPLE 30-HOME RUN, 30-STEAL SEASONS. FROM 1990 THROUGH 1997, ONLY ONE PLAYER (SAMMY SOSA IN 1995) HAS MORE STEALS AND MORE HOME RUNS THAN BARRY BONDS IN THE SAME SEASON. FOR AN EVEN BETTER GAUGE OF HIS UNIQUE COMBINATION

"Every one of those players, like Barry Bonds, Hank Aaron, all those top, special guys have a tremendous brain, a visual system that is able to see beyond what the average person can see. They have the ability for the brain to be in alpha state for performance, a state of euphoria where the ball looks larger than normal and seems to be traveling at a slower speed. Michael Jordan had the same thing in basketball. The great ones get in that state more often. Plus, they are geniuses in their field. Ted Williams was a genius at hitting. I asked him once what percentage of the time did he know what a pitcher was going to throw. He said 75 percent of the time."

★ SYD THRIFT

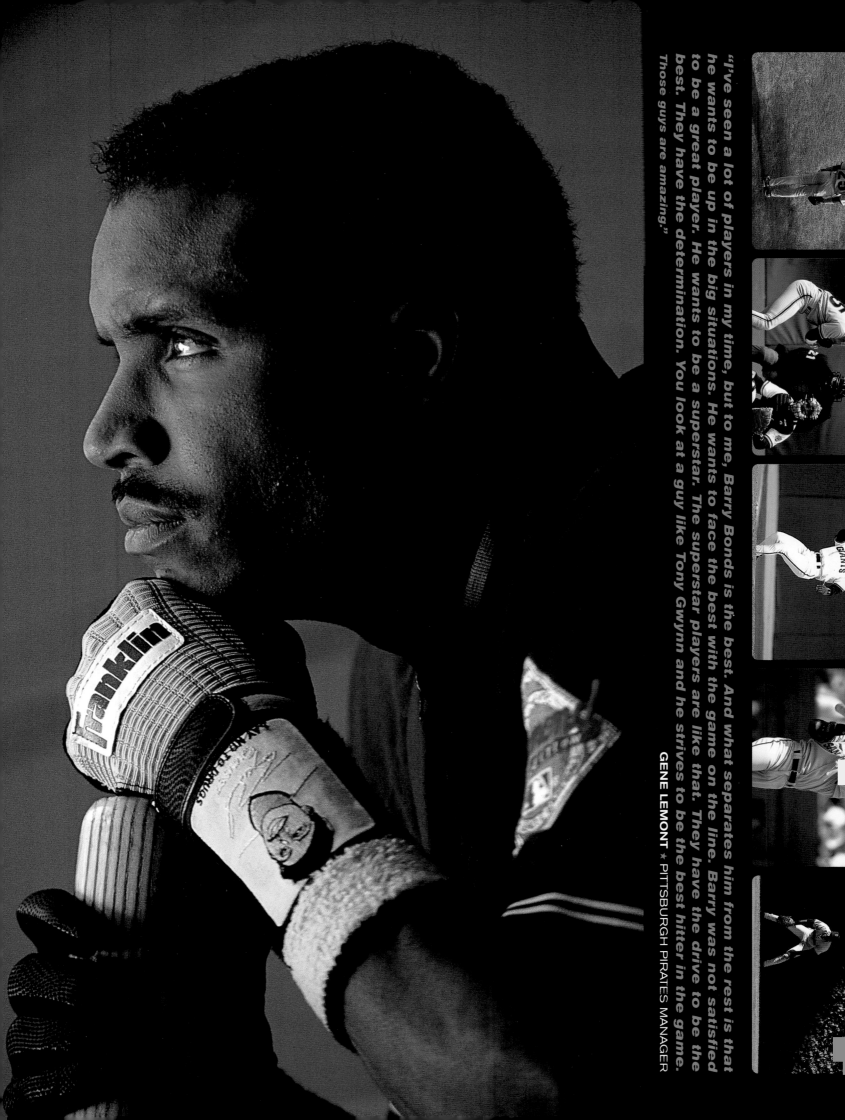

"I've seen a lot of players in my time, but to me, Barry Bonds is the best. And what separates him from the rest is that he wants to be up in the big situations. He wants to face the best with the game on the line. Barry was not satisfied to be a great player. He wants to be a superstar. The superstar players are like that. They have the drive to be the best. They have the determination. You look at a guy like Tony Gwynn and he strives to be the best hitter in the game. Those guys are amazing."

GENE LEMONT ★ PITTSBURGH PIRATES MANAGER

★ "THERE WERE ONLY 60,65 STARTING PITCHERS IN ALL OF BASEBALL. NOW THERE ARE 200 GUYS STARTING GAMES. IT WAS A LOT TOUGHER TO HIT THEN THAN IT IS NOW. THAT MIGHT SOUND OLD-SCHOOL, BUT EVERY TEAM HAD FOUR GOOD STARTING PITCHERS. I MEAN EVERY TEAM. IF YOU ARE COMPARING JOE DIMAGGIO TO GUYS IN TODAY'S GAME, CAREER-WISE HE STRUCK OUT EIGHT MORE TIMES THAN THE NUMBER OF HOME RUNS HE HIT. IF YOU'RE LOOKING FOR STATISTICS, THAT'S AS GOOD AS IT GETS. HE STRUCK OUT 13 TIMES THE YEAR OF THE STREAK. THAT'S A GOOD WEEK FOR A GREAT PLAYER TODAY.

JIM FREGOSI, LIKE DIMAGGIO, A SAN FRANCISCO NATIVE
OF ITALIAN DESCENT, IS MANAGER OF THE TORONTO BLUE JAYS

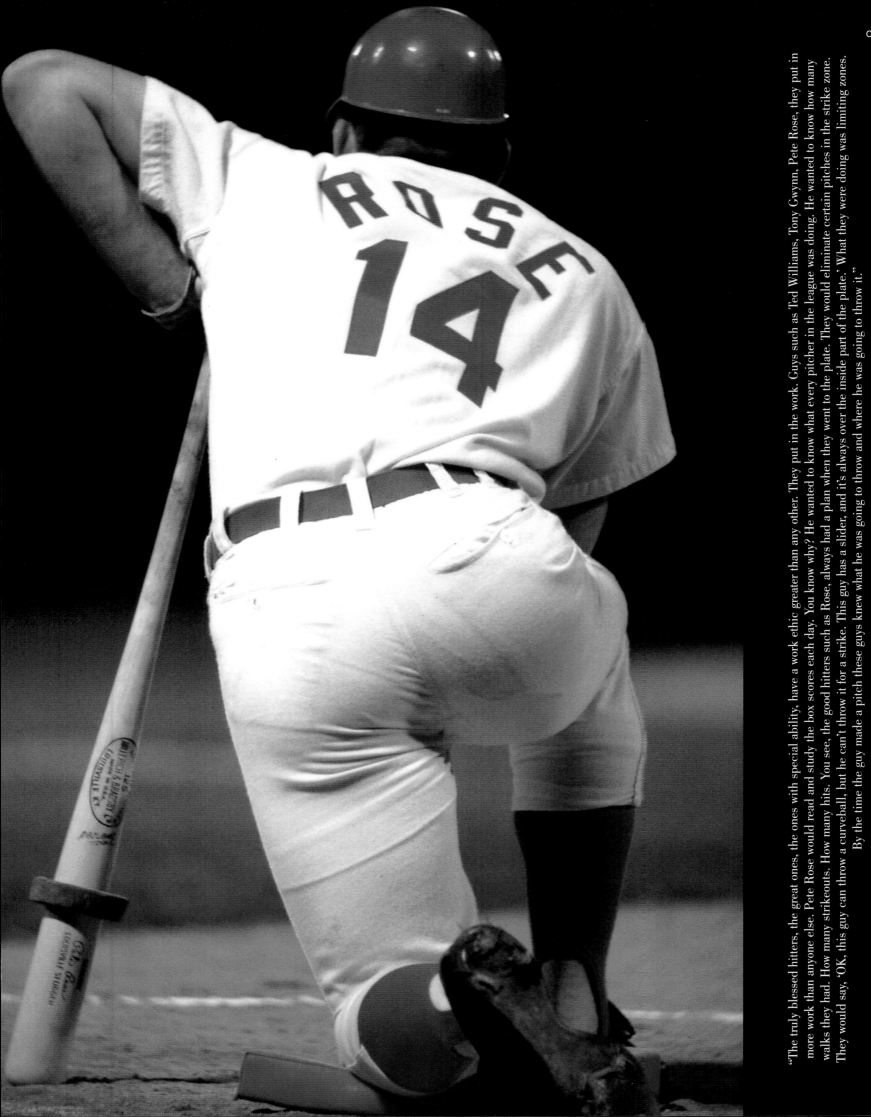

"The truly blessed hitters, the great ones, the ones with special ability, have a work ethic greater than any other. They put in the work. Guys such as Ted Williams, Tony Gwynn, Pete Rose, they put in more work than anyone else. Pete Rose would read and study the box scores each day. You know why? He wanted to know what every pitcher in the league was doing. He wanted to know how many walks they had. How many strikeouts. How many hits. You see, the good hitters such as Rose, always had a plan when they went to the plate. They would eliminate certain pitches in the strike zone. They would say, 'OK, this guy can throw a curveball, but he can't throw it for a strike. This guy has a slider, and it's always over the inside part of the plate.' What they were doing was limiting zones. By the time the guy made a pitch these guys knew what he was going to throw and where he was going to throw it."

DEACON JONES ★ SPECIAL ASSIGNMENT SCOUT FOR THE BALTIMORE ORIOLES

"I IDOLIZED THREE GUYS WHEN I WAS GROWING UP,

JOE DIMAGGIO, STAN MUSIAL AND TED WILLIAMS.

OF THE THREE I THOUGHT JOE HAD THE BEST ALL-AROUND GAME. HE COULD
HIT, THROW, RUN AND FIELD. I WANTED TO PATTERN MYSELF AFTER HIM."

★

WILLIE MAYS

"THE GREATEST TOOLS I HAVE SEEN IN ALL MY YEARS OF SCOUTING BELONG TO KEN GRIFFEY JR. HE'S THE BEST ALL-AROUND PLAYER I HAVE SEEN. HE CAN RUN. HE CAN THROW. HE'S THE WHOLE PACKAGE.

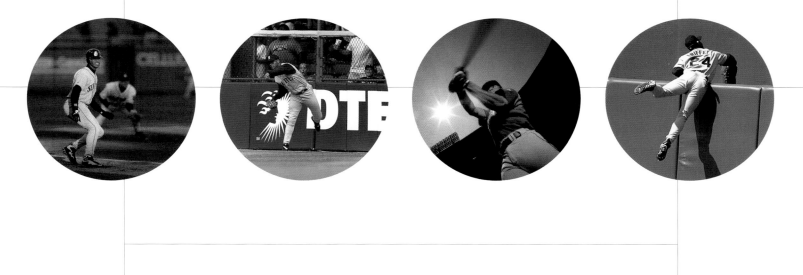

THE ONLY ONE CLOSE TO HIM IS VLADIMIR GUERRERO OF THE EXPOS. EVERYTHING HE DOES IS SO EXPLOSIVE. BUT GRIFFEY IS THE BEST I HAVE EVER SEEN. WE HAVE THIS GRADING SCALE OF 20 TO 80 AND HE'S THE HIGHEST RATED PLAYER MAYBE IN BASEBALL HISTORY. HE HAS EVERYTHING. HE HAS THE POWER. THE SPEED. HE CAN THROW. HE CAN RUN. HE CAN FIELD. I NEVER SAW WILLIE MAYS PLAY, BUT I CAN'T IMAGINE ANYONE WOULD BE RATED HIGHER ACROSS THE BOARD THAN GRIFFEY. AND REMEMBER, THIS GUY ALREADY HAD ALL THESE TOOLS AT THE AGE OF 18. HE JUST REFINED THEM, THAT'S ALL."

OMAR MINAYA ★ NEW YORK METS ASSISTANT GENERAL MANAGER,
WHO SIGNED CHICAGO CUBS OUTFIELDER SAMMY SOSA.

"HE'S STILL THE BEST LEFT-HANDED HITTER I'VE EVER SEEN IN MY LIFE. EVERY AT-BAT WAS WHAT I CALL A BIG-LEAGUE AT-BAT. HE NEVER GAVE IN TO ANYTHING. AND HE ALWAYS HIT THE BALL HARD. THE THING ABOUT BRETT THAT STICKS OUT THE MOST WAS THAT EVEN WHEN HE WASN'T FEELING THE BEST WITH HIS KNEES, HE WENT ALL OUT EVERY TIME HE HIT THE BALL. GEORGE BRETT WAS NOT GOING TO BE JOGGING TO FIRST BASE. NO SIR. BRETT'S SINGLES WERE SINGLES ONLY BECAUSE YOU STOPPED HIM. HE ALWAYS MADE THAT HARD TURN LOOKING TO GO FOR TWO. IF HE SAW A WEAKNESS IN YOUR GAME, HE POUNCED ON YOU. HE NOT ONLY BEAT YOU WITH GRACE, BUT AT THE SAME TIME HE WAS OLD SCHOOL. I NEVER SAW GEORGE BRETT WEAR BATTING GLOVES. NOT ONCE. HE JUST PUT ON THAT GAME-FACE AND WAS READY TO GO."

THAD BOSLEY ★ FORMER TEAMMATE OF BRETT IN KANSAS CITY

WHEN GEORGE BRETT WON THE AMERICAN LEAGUE BATTING TITLE IN 1990, HE BECAME THE FIRST PLAYER – AND TO THIS POINT, THE ONLY ONE – TO WIN BATTING TITLES IN THREE DIFFERENT DECADES.

He previously had led the American League in batting average in 1976 and in 1980. Simply winning three batting titles is a great feat — not as apparent from the surprising number of players who have done it (17) as it is from their names: Lajoie, Wagner, Cobb, Heilmann, Hornsby, Waner, Musial, Williams, Clemente, Yastrzemski, Oliva, Rose, Carew, Madlock, Boggs, Gwynn and Brett.

Brett was a 12-time All-Star and he was named American League MVP in 1980. He was a good enough fielder to win the Gold Glove in 1985. And he was an outstanding postseason performer for the Royals, batting .337 with 10 home runs in 43 postseason games.

But even if Brett didn't need a signature achievement, he had a legitimate one: He is the only player to have challenged the .400 mark seriously since Ted

Williams batted .406 in 1941. Brett batted .390 in 1980 and he maintained an average in the .400s as late as Sept. 4. To put that in perspective: Over nearly 60 years since Williams' milestone, only one other player carried a .400 average beyond mid-July. John Olerud made it to Aug. 2 in 1993; other than that, the latest date was July 18, by Larry Walker in 1997.

Brett's .390 mark for the season was the second highest in the post-.406 era, and even the higher mark has an asterisk. Tony Gwynn batted .394 in 1994, the season shortened by a players' strike. Technically, Gwynn qualified for and won the NL batting title; but his total of 475 plate appearances is 27 less than he would have needed to qualify in a full season. It's also worth noting that Brett's .466 batting average with runners in scoring position in 1980 was the highest mark of the last 25 years.

"DRIVING INTO THE PARKING LOT AT CLEAR CREEK HIGH SCHOOL, I NOTICED THAT ALVIN (TEXAS) HIGH SCHOOL WAS PLAYING IN THE GAME THAT WAS UNDER WAY. AS I SETTLED INTO MY SEAT, THE ALVIN COACH WAS MAKING A PITCHING CHANGE AND UP TO THE MOUND WALKED A GANGLY, AWKWARD-LOOKING 6-FOOT KID WHO COULD NOT HAVE WEIGHED MORE THAN 150 POUNDS. I HAD SEEN A THOUSAND LIKE HIM DURING MY TRAVELS. *HE WAS AN ORDINARY, UNPOLISHED KID WHO LOOKED LIKE HE WAS MAYBE 12 OR 13 YEARS OLD.* I FIGURED HE WAS PROBABLY A SOPHOMORE OR A JUNIOR, MAYBE 15 OR 16. THERE WAS NOTHING REMARKABLE ABOUT THIS YOUNGSTER AT ALL. NOTHING UNUSUAL THAT WOULD HAVE PROVIDED THE LEAST HINT THAT WHAT I WAS ABOUT TO WITNESS WAS NOT A ONE-IN-ONE-THOUSAND, NOT ONE-IN-A-MILLION, BUT *A ONCE-IN-A-LIFETIME EXPERIENCE.*

"BEFORE I COULD SAY MY HELLOS TO THE PEOPLE I KNEW, I GLANCED TOWARD THE MOUND AS *THE YOUNG PITCHER WOUND UP AND FIRED. I COULD NOT BELIEVE* WHAT I HAD JUST SEEN. HOW IN THE WORLD COULD ANYONE THAT KID'S SIZE THROW LIKE THAT? HE WOUND UP AGAIN AND THREW ANOTHER PITCH THAT LOOKED LIKE IT HAD COME FROM A ROCKET LAUNCHER, THIS TIME ON THE OUTSIDE CORNER OF THE PLATE FOR ANOTHER STRIKE.

"YOU COULD HEAR IT SIZZLE LIKE A THICK OF HAM FRYING ON A RED-HOT GRIDDLE AS IT ROARED TOWARD THE PLATE. WHEN THE BALL SLAMMED INTO THE CATCHER'S GLOVE, THE SOUND REMINDED ME OF A RIFLE SHOT.

"I DIDN'T EVEN KNOW THIS KID'S NAME, BUT THAT *GOD HAD RICHLY BLESSED THIS YOUNG MAN* WAS BLATANTLY OBVIOUS. THAT FASTBALL OF HIS WAS UNBELIEVABLE. IT WAS THE FASTEST I EVER HAD SEEN ANYWHERE. MAJOR LEAGUES, MINOR LEAGUES, ANYWHERE.

"IF A BALL IS COMING IN STRAIGHT, I DON'T CARE HOW FAST IT'S MOVING. PROFESSIONAL HITTERS EVENTUALLY WILL CATCH UP WITH IT AND KNOCK THE BALL ALL OVER THE PARK. BUT THIS FASTBALL HAD LIFE. IT JUMPED OFF HIS HAND AND APPEARED TO HOP AS IT HURTLED TOWARD HOME PLATE.

"UNLIKE SO MANY OTHER DAYS WHEN I HAD BEEN BORED BY A LACK OF TALENT AT THE BALLPARK, ON THIS DAY I COULDN'T WAIT TO GET HOME TO FILL OUT MY SCOUTING REPORT. I GOT EXCITED AGAIN WHEN I SAT DOWN IN MY OFFICE AND BEGAN TO WRITE. I'LL NEVER FORGET MY COMMENTS:

BEST ARM I EVER SAW ANYWHERE IN MY LIFE.
EVERY TIME I SAW NOLAN, I WOULD WRITE THE SAME THING. BEST ARM I EVER SAW ANYWHERE IN MY LIFE.

"I FELT QUALIFIED TO MAKE THAT JUDGMENT BECAUSE BESIDES MY PROFESSIONAL EXPERIENCE AND HAVING PLAYED WITH WARREN SPAHN AND LEW BURDETTE, I HAD SEEN TWO OF THE BEST FASTBALL PITCHERS IN THE NATIONAL LEAGUE AT THE TIME – JIM MALONEY OF THE CINCINNATI REDS AND DICK "TURK" FARRELL OF THE HOUSTON ASTROS. BOTH OF THOSE MEN WERE BIG AND STRONG AND COULD THROW HARD.

NOLAN RYAN,
AS A JUNIOR IN HIGH SCHOOL, WAS FASTER BY FAR."

SCOUT JOHN "RED" MURFF
SIGNED NOLAN RYAN TO HIS
FIRST PROFESSIONAL CCNTRACT.

HITTING

"EVERY TIME I STEPPED UP TO THE PLATE WITH A BAT IN MY HANDS, I FELT SORRY FOR THEM." ★ **ROGERS HORNSBY** HAS THE SECOND HIGHEST CAREER BATTING AVERAGE IN MAJOR LEAGUE BASEBALL HISTORY (.358)

OR AVERAGE

JOE JACKSON   ROD CAREW   TRIS SPEAKER   PAUL MOLITOR   PETE ROSE

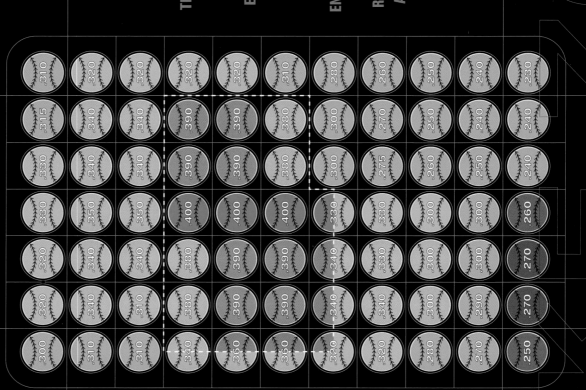

"I used to ask myself all the time, why are these guys great hitters? What do they do that I can't do? Then I realized that the great ones, the truly great ones, simply are more prepared than the rest. You take Ted Williams. Ted Williams would take pitches in batting practice. I'm serious. Sure, he could hit any of those pitches, but if they were out of the strike zone, he would take them. I asked Williams why he would do that and he told me,

'I'M STILL HITTING EVEN THOUGH I'M TAKING A PITCH. I'M DEFINING MY STRIKE ZONE.' You have to have a good feeling for that strike zone."

★

DEACON JONES
SPECIAL ASSIGNMENT SCOUT FOR THE BALTIMORE ORIOLES

TED WILLIAMS' STRIKE ZONE

EVEN THE GREATEST HITTERS EXIST IN THE SHADOW OF TED WILLIAMS. DESPITE LEADING THE LEAGUE IN WALKS EIGHT TIMES AND MISSING VIRTUALLY FIVE ENTIRE SEASONS TO MILITARY SERVICE, THE "SPLENDID SPLINTER" REMAINS THE MODEL TO WHICH ALL OTHERS ARE COMPARED. THE CHART IS AN ENLARGED VERSION OF WILLIAMS' STRIKE ZONE. THE NUMBER ON EACH BALL REPRESENTS WILLIAMS' LIKELY BATTING AVERAGE IF EVERY PITCH CROSSED THE PLATE AT THAT LOCATION.

TY COBB'S BATTING TIPS

FROM A MAY 18, 1938 LETTER TO ROOKIE RIGHT-HANDED HITTING OUTFIELDER SAM CHAPMAN THAT FIRST APPEARED IN PRINT IN 1947.

1 **Don't grip your bat at the very end;** leave, say, an inch or two. **Also, leave at least an inch or more space between your hands;** that gives you balance and control of bat and also keeps hands from interfering with each other during swing.

2 Take position at plate, especially against right-hand pitchers, **back of plate;** and against a man with a real curve, **you can stay on back line of batting box.** Now try to hit to right-center.

3 **Don't slug at full speed; learn to meet them firmly** and you will be surprised at the results.

4 Now, to hit as I ask, to right-center or center, **you stand away from plate** the distance you can see with mind's eye that you can hit the ball that curves on inside corner, to center. This distance away from plate will allow you to hit the outside ball to right. In other words, protect the plate both on inside pitches and outside.

5 Remember, **the plate is the pitcher's objective and he has to come to it.** I use "back of plate" expression to mean towards the catcher, away from plate to denote distance from plate towards outside of box. Now, **use a slightly closed stance and keep a little more weight on your front foot than back.** That gives you balance and won't pull you away from curves. You are always in position to give maximum drive.

6 **Keep your left elbow cocked on level with your hands or even higher.** Never let your elbow down below the hands and keep your hands always well away from your body – keep pushing them out, even with your body or back.

7 **Keep your back leg straight.** Of course, if you put your weight more on the front leg, then the back leg will be straight.

8 **If high fastballs inside really bother you:** Crouch over from waist and pass them up. Don't bite, in other words. In crouching, you make the pitcher throw lower, which forces him away from the position that bothers you. But I think with the instructions I have given, you will hit them wherever they pitch.

9 **Don't pull a curveball from a right-hander.** The ball is revolving away from you. Hit with the revolution and to right field.

10 **Against a speedy left-hander, don't pull.** Use same stance I have given you, and when he throws you his curve, knock him down with it or you will naturally pull it, as the ball is breaking in to you. **But against left-hander of fair speed,** move up in the box, also closer to plate, and **pull this style of pitching.**

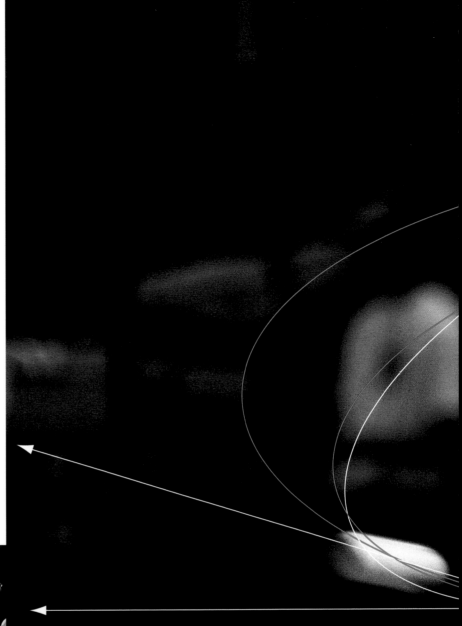

TONY GWYNN, PERHAPS THE GREATEST HITTER OF HIS GENERATION, STARTED HITTING WITH POWER HIS LAST FEW YEARS AFTER A HEART-TO-HEART TALK WITH HALL OF FAMER TED WILLIAMS. WILLIAMS, WHO WAS BORN IN SAN DIEGO, PLAYED HIS FINAL GAME IN 1960, THE YEAR GWYNN WAS BORN.

THE TWO HAVE BECOME CLOSE, WITH GWYNN HOLDING WILLIAMS STEADY WHILE HE THREW OUT THE CEREMONIAL FIRST PITCH AT THE 1999 ALL-STAR GAME.

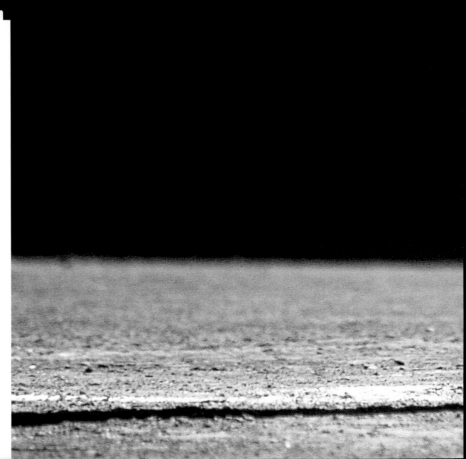

"We talked for two hours," Gwynn said of his 1996 conversation with Williams. "He kept saying, that I had to meet the inside pitch in front of the plate. He's yelling at me, 'You have got to turn on it. You have to let it go. Let it go.'

"Now I know what he was talking about. I always liked to back the ball up. The longer you can look at a pitch, the better your chances of hitting it. If you just let your swing go, your chances of not hitting it or pulling it foul are greater. So you have got to have confidence to turn on a pitch, to trust letting it go.

"Hitting is all about being comfortable at the plate. I have learned to get comfortable hitting this way. I have learned to let it go, like Ted said."

GWYNN, WHO SLAPPED HIS 3,000TH HIT IN 1999, STILL REMEMBERS HIS FIRST MAJOR LEAGUE GAME WHEN HE PRODUCED TWO HITS AGAINST THE PHILADELPHIA PHILLIES. THE FIRST HIT WAS A DOUBLE AND THE PHILLIES FIRST BASEMAN, TRAILING ON THE PLAY, STOPPED BEHIND GWYNN AND YELLED: "HEY, KID, WHAT ARE YOU TRYING TO DO, CATCH ME IN ONE NIGHT?" THE FIRST BASEMAN WAS PETE ROSE, BASEBALL'S ALL-TIME HITS LEADER.

"His great concentration separated him from the rest. If he got a hit the first time up, he would want to get a second hit. If he got a second hit, he would want a third hit. And when he got a third hit, you just knew he was going to go four for four. He was unique, boy. Some guys get two hits and say, 'That's good enough.' But not him. I never once saw him give away an at-bat."

JOE GARAGIOLA ★ FORMER ST. LOUIS CARDINALS CATCHER

"WHAT'S THE BEST WAY TO PITCH TO STAN MUSIAL?

THAT'S EASY. WALK HIM
AND THEN TRY TO PICK HIM
OFF FIRST BASE."

JOE GARAGIOLA

SINCE THE CURRENT VOTING PROCEDURE WAS ESTABLISHED IN 1931, JOE MORGAN IS THE ONLY SECOND BASEMAN TO WIN MORE THAN ONE MOST VALUABLE PLAYER AWARD. MORGAN EARNED HIS PAIR OF MVP AWARDS IN 1975 AND 1976 AND SOME THOUGHT HE WAS DESERVING OF THE AWARD IN 1973 AND 1974 AS WELL WHEN HE PLACED FOURTH AND EIGHTH RESPECTIVELY.

Even before 1931, only one other second baseman won two MVP awards. Rogers Hornsby was named the National League MVP in 1925 and 1929 — a different award, under a different voting procedure than the one in practice for the past 69 years. (For the record, other second basemen to win the award since then are Frankie Frisch, Charlie Gehringer, Joe Gordon, Jackie Robinson, Nellie Fox and Ryne Sandberg.)

Morgan's MVP awards are so significant because the concept of his value to his teams often is discussed. *Total Baseball* referred to Morgan as the "generator" of the Big Red Machine. Morgan's arrival in Cincinnati in 1972 followed the team's disappointing fourth-place finish a year earlier and generally is considered to be the move that turned the Reds back into the Big Red Machine — a far better version, in fact, than the team that reached the World Series in 1970. But Morgan's value wasn't demonstrated only when he joined the Reds. Every team for which he subsequently played also improved when he arrived:

TEAM	BEFORE MORGAN		
	YEAR	W-L	PCT.
REDS	1971	79-83	.488
ASTROS	1979	89-73	.549
GIANTS	1980	75-86	.466
PHILLIES	1982	89-73	.549
ATHLETICS	1983	74-88	.457
TOTALS		406-403	.502

"WHEN YOU'RE A BASE STEALER, YOU CAUSE THINGS TO HAPPEN. THE PITCHER WORRIES ABOUT YOU, THE CATCHER KNOWS YOU'RE THERE AND THE INFIELDERS KNOW YOU'RE THERE. YOU CAN DO A LOT OF THINGS TO THE DEFENSE."

JOE MORGAN ★ *NEW YORK TIMES*, 1975

MORGAN'S FIRST SEASON

YEAR	W-L	PCT.	DIFF.
1972	95-59	.617	+20
1980	93-70	.571	+3.5
1981	56-55	.505	+6
1983	90-72	.556	+1
1984	77-85	.475	+3
	411-341	.547	+33

Incidentally, in four of those five moves the team that Morgan left posted a worse record after losing him. Only the 1972 Astros improved their record after Morgan's departure. Even including that team's gain, the five teams fell by an average of six victories.

What's truly impressive about those figures is what they do not show. All but one season of Morgan's spectacular six-year span from 1972 to 1977 has been excluded.

During that period, Morgan won two MVP awards and five Gold Gloves. He led the majors in runs, walks and on-base average, and he ranked second to Lou Brock in stolen bases. But he wasn't just a table-setter. Morgan hit 130 home runs for the six seasons — just four fewer than Tony Perez — and he ranked 11th in extra-base hits. In 1976, he also ranked second in the majors in RBIs. His slugging percentage for the period was .495 — five points higher than Reggie Jackson's career mark!

HITTING

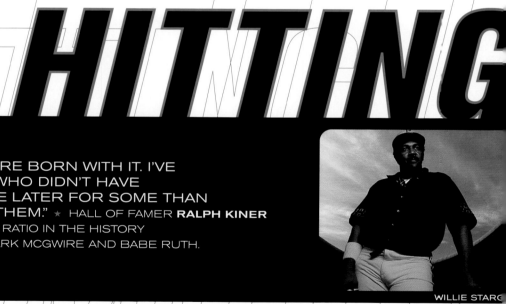

WILLIE STARG[...]

"POWER IS GOD-GIVEN. YOU ARE BORN WITH IT. I'VE NEVER SEEN ANYONE DEVELOP IT WHO DIDN'T HAVE IT TO BEGIN WITH. IT MIGHT COME LATER FOR SOME THAN OTHERS, BUT THEY ALWAYS HAD IT IN THEM." ★ HALL OF FAMER **RALPH KINER** HAS THE THIRD-HIGHEST HOME RUN PER AT BAT RATIO IN THE HISTORY OF THE GAME, RANKING BEHIND ONLY MARK MCGWIRE AND BABE RUTH.

FOR POWER

REGGIE JACKSON   EDDIE MATHEWS   SAMMY SOSA   CARL YASTRZEMSKI

"One day in Pittsburgh at Three Rivers Stadium I heard the crack of the bat at three in the afternoon. I went out there and Mike Schmidt was hitting and Del Unser was standing by the cage. What Schmidt was working on was to not hit the ball in the air unless it was a line drive. Every time he hit a fly ball he would get upset. He broke some home run record one night in Pittsburgh and *THAT BALL THAT HE BROKE THE RECORD WITH, HE HIT IT ON A LINE DRIVE.*

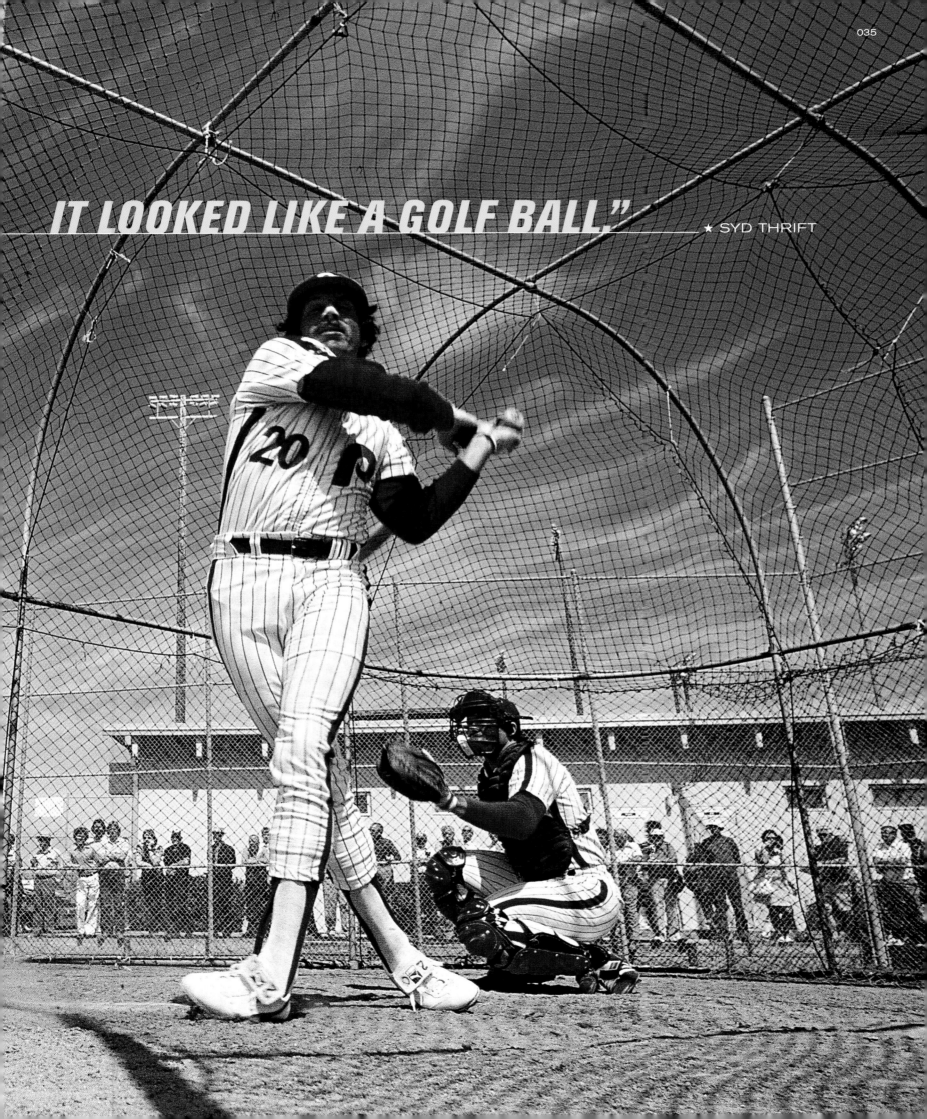

IT LOOKED LIKE A GOLF BALL." ★ SYD THRIFT

I WAS SITTING ON THE SIDE AT THE 1999 HOME RUN DERBY

AND I WAS JUST AMAZED AT WHAT MARK MCGWIRE WAS ABLE TO DO. HE JUST KEPT HITTING THESE TOWERING DRIVES INTO THE LIGHT TOWERS AND THEY KEPT DISAPPEARING. THE BALLS JUST KEPT DISAPPEARING. IT WAS AMAZING. IT'S IMPOSSIBLE TO HIT THE BALL THAT FAR. HE WAS MAKING BALLS DISAPPEAR LIKE MAGIC. I NEVER HAVE SEEN ANY-BODY HIT THE BALL THE WAY HE DOES. I NEVER

SAW RUTH PLAY BUT I CAN'T IMAGINE HIM HITTING THEM ANY FARTHER THAN MCGWIRE. I WOULD STILL HAVE TO PUT MY MONEY ON KEN GRIFFEY JR. AS HAVING THE BEST CHANCE TO BREAK MY HOME RUN RECORD. BUT I CERTAINLY WOULDN'T COUNT OUT MCGWIRE. NO SIR. IF HE KEEPS GOING AT THE PACE HE HAS BEEN GOING THE PAST FEW YEARS, BREAKING THE RECORD IS A DEFINITE POSSIBILITY.

★ HANK AARON

HOW TO HIT HOME RUNS:

I SWING AS HARD AS I CAN AND I TRY TO SWING RIGHT THROUGH THE BALL. IN BOXING, YOUR FIST USUALLY STOPS WHEN YOU HIT A MAN, BUT IT'S POSSIBLE TO HIT SO HARD THAT YOUR FIST DOESN'T STOP. I TRY TO FOLLOW THROUGH IN THE SAME WAY. THE HARDER YOU GRIP THE BAT, THE MORE YOU CAN SWING IT THROUGH THE BALL AND THE FARTHER THE BALL WILL GO. I SWING BIG, WITH EVERYTHING I HAVE. I HIT BIG OR I MISS BIG. I LIKE TO LIVE AS BIG AS I CAN.

BABE RUTH ★ QUOTED BY WILLIAM SAFIRE AND LEONARD SAFIRE IN *Words of Wisdom*

"I think McGwire hits the ball farther than anyone I've ever seen. But if Hank Greenberg and Jimmie Foxx hit a similar ball they would have hit it just as far. The equipment is different now. It's not the same ball."

★

HALL OF FAMER RALPH KINER

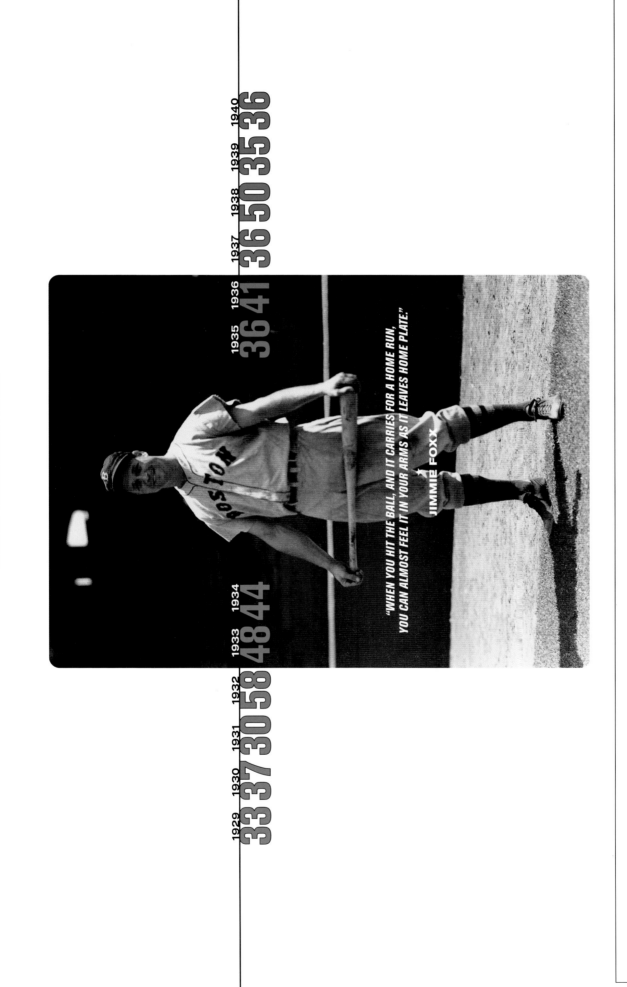

"WHEN YOU HIT THE BALL, AND IT CARRIES FOR A HOME RUN, YOU CAN ALMOST FEEL IT IN YOUR ARMS AS IT LEAVES HOME PLATE."

JIMMIE FOXX

1929 1930 1931 1932 1933 1934 1935 1936 1937 1938 1939 1940
33 37 30 58 48 44 36 41 36 50 35 36

JIMMIE FOXX HIT AT LEAST 30 HOME RUNS IN 12 CONSECUTIVE SEASONS FROM 1929 THROUGH 1940, THE LONGEST SUCH STREAK IN MAJOR LEAGUE HISTORY. HE ALSO DROVE IN 1,403 RUNS DURING THE 1930S, THE HIGHEST TOTAL OF ANY PLAYER IN ANY DECADE. **FOXX HIT 534 CAREER HOME RUNS, SECOND ON THE ALL-TIME LIST BEHIND BABE RUTH WHEN HE RETIRED IN 1945.** BARRING INJURY, KEN GRIFFEY JR. SHOULD BECOME THE **YOUNGEST PLAYER TO HIT 400 HOME RUNS SINCE FOXX (30 YEARS 8 MONTHS).** GRIFFEY HAD 395 HOME RUNS WITH TWO WEEKS REMAINING IN THE 1999 SEASON AND DIDN'T TURN 30 UNTIL NOV. 21, 1999.

"NO ONE WAS MENTALLY TOUGHER THAN FRANK ROBINSON. IF YOU KNOCKED HIM ON HIS BUTT THREE TIMES IN A ROW AND CAME ANYWHERE NEAR THE PLATE THE FOURTH TIME, HE WOULD HIT IT A MILE."

★

SEATTLE MARINERS PITCHING COACH **STAN WILLIAMS**

FRANK ROBINSON
HR   RBI
TRIPLE CROWN
'66
BA .316   HR 49   RBI 122
AVERAGE

FRANK ROBINSON MIGHT BE ONE OF THE MOST UNDER-APPRECIATED SUPERSTARS OF THE CENTURY. HE NOT ONLY WON THE TRIPLE CROWN IN 1966, BUT ROBINSON WAS ONE OF THE THREE DOMINANT HITTERS IN THE CROWN CATEGORIES THROUGHOUT THE 1960S. THERE WERE 27 SEASONS OF .300 BA/30 HR/100 RBI DURING THE '60S; ONLY THREE PLAYERS HAD MORE THAN TWO: ROBINSON, WILLIE MAYS AND HANK AARON HAD FOUR EACH.

"Frank Robinson could do it all. He had no fear. He would stand on top of that plate and almost dare you to pitch inside. He could hit and he could throw with the best of them. My favorite story about Frank is when he was coming up to Cincinnati after barn-storming in Savannah, Ga. He got beaned by Camilo Pascual. He hit Frank so hard that the ball hit his head and bounced all the way to the screen. And you know what? He was back in the lineup and playing the very next day."

FORMER ST. LOUIS CARDINALS AND TEXAS RANGERS MANAGER **WHITEY HERZOG**

"We didn't always keep accurate records. Some days we would have a guy who kept score, some days we wouldn't. That year, I played with Josh Gibson, and they were talking about what a great hitter he was and how many home runs he hit. So I said that I was going to keep track of how many he hit and he hit 72 that year. But, in the records, you'll only see 55. Like when I stole all those bases, they only have a record of 91. Sometimes we played in parks that weren't fenced in. Josh would hit a ball 450 feet, but somebody would be standing out there, and they would catch it. If we had played in the major league parks that were fenced in, Josh probably would have hit more than 100 home runs." ★ **JAMES "COOL PAPA" BELL** QUOTED BY JOHN M. COATES, OCTOBER 1973/BLACK SPORTS.

WE DIDN'T ALWAYS KEEP ACCURATE RECORDS.

JOSH GIBSON ★ CATCHER

UPON HIS RETURN FROM MILITARY SERVICE,
WILLIE MAYS BECAME PART OF THE LEGENDARY TRIO
OF NEW YORK CENTER FIELDERS IMMORTALIZED AS

WILLIE, MICKEY AND THE DUKE.

ALL THREE RANKED IN THE MAJOR LEAGUE TOP
10 IN HOME RUNS FROM 1954 TO 1957;
AND WITH ONE EXCEPTION THEY RANKED AMONG
THE TOP 20 IN RBIS FOR ALL FOUR YEARS.

HOME RUNS

SNIDER 165 ★ MAYS 163 ★ MANTLE 150

From 1954 to 1957, Duke Snider, Willie Mays and Mickey Mantle ranked 1-2-3 in home runs and all three ranked among the top seven in RBIs (Snider, 1st/459; Mantle, 5th/425; Mays, 7th/418).

4 YEAR POWER NUMBERS

4 YEAR POWER NUMBERS

MANTLE

SNIDER

MAYS

★ NOTE ★
IT WAS SNIDER WHO POSTED THE BEST
OFFENSIVE NUMBERS DURING THAT PERIOD, SURPASSING
THOSE OF HIS MORE HERALDED PARTNERS.

540 08/03/62
On to left-field roof at Tiger Stadium off Jim Bunning. First onto the roof in 24 years. Estimated 540 feet.

522 06/03/67
Hit first homer to left-field upper deck at Metropolitan Stadium (1 of 2 ever) off Lew Burdette. Estimated 522 feet.

520 09/11/60
Hit facing of left-field roof (80 feet high) off Bill Fischer. No one to that point had hit a ball onto this roof since Metropolitan Stadium was built in 1938. Estimated 520 feet.

510 06/04/67
Off facing of left-center-field upper deck at Metropolitan Stadium off Jack Sanford. Estimated 510 feet.

500 08/06/60
Hit rising live drive off Herb Score that struck steel girder in left-field upper deck at Comiskey Park and bounced back to shortstop position. Estimated 500 feet. Killebrew considers this one of the hardest balls he ever hit.

500 07/01/72
Left field roof at Comiskey Park off Dave Lemonds. 13th time in 45 years ball off the roof. Estimated 500 feet.

500 05/17/64
Left-center-field light tower 375 feet away and 70 feet above ground at Fenway Park off Dave Morehead. Estimated 500 feet

490 08/26/63
Fourth row of center-field upper deck at Robert F. Kennedy Stadium off Ed Roebuck. 490 feet.

480 06/19/59
28 rows into the distant left-field bleachers at Griffith Stadium off Paul Foytack. Estimated 480 feet.

476 06/20/66
Hit 476-foot measured home run to base of A-frame scoreboard at Anaheim Stadium in left-center before stadium was enclosed. Off George Brunet.

ON JUNE 3, 1967 MINNESOTA TWINS OWNER CALVIN GRIFFITH RETIRED SEAT NO. 9, ROW 5 OF SECTION 34 OF THE SECOND DECK OF METROPOLITAN STADIUM. HARMON KILLEBREW'S HOME RUN THE DAY BEFORE WAS REPUTED TO BE THE LONGEST IN STADIUM HISTORY – A SHOT ESTIMATED AT 520 FEET. THE FOLLOWING DAY KILLEBREW HIT A "LINE DRIVE" THAT TRAVELED AN ESTIMATED 500 FEET.

471 04/30/61
Hit center-field backdrop beyond wall at Metropolitan Stadium off Chicago's Bob Shaw. Estimated 471 feet.

470 04/24/64
Longest home run (to that point) ever measured at Baltimore's Memorial Stadium. Off Milt Pappas. Ball cleared hedges in left-center.

"I see all these guys lifting weights, I was told to never do that. All I did was play baseball and hunt and fish. Of course, I had other jobs in the winter, too. I sold men's clothing, fed cattle and worked for the gas company. Somebody asked me last year how many homers I think I could hit against today's pitching. I said, "Oh, I think I could hit 30 or so." And the guy says, "That's not very many." I said, "Well, you have got to remember that I'm 62 years old." ★ HARMON KILLEBREW

KILLEBREW BOMBS KILLEBREW BOMBS

12

"YOU'RE ALONE IN A SEA OF ENEMIES. THE ONLY WAY YOU CAN HOLD YOUR OWN
IS BY ARROGANCE, THE ABILITY TO STAND BEFORE THE CROWD.
EVERY TIME YOU GET THROWN OUT, YOU'VE GOT TO BELIEVE THAT SOMEBODY
OWES YOU FOUR OR FIVE STEALS. THEN YOU'VE GOT TO GO OUT AND GET THEM."

★ **LOU BROCK** NEW YORK TIMES, 1982

SPEED

LOU BROCK   JACKIE ROBINSON   PETE ROSE   MICKEY MANTLE   RICKEY HENDERSON

STOLEN

50 BASES IN 12 CONSECUTIVE SEASONS

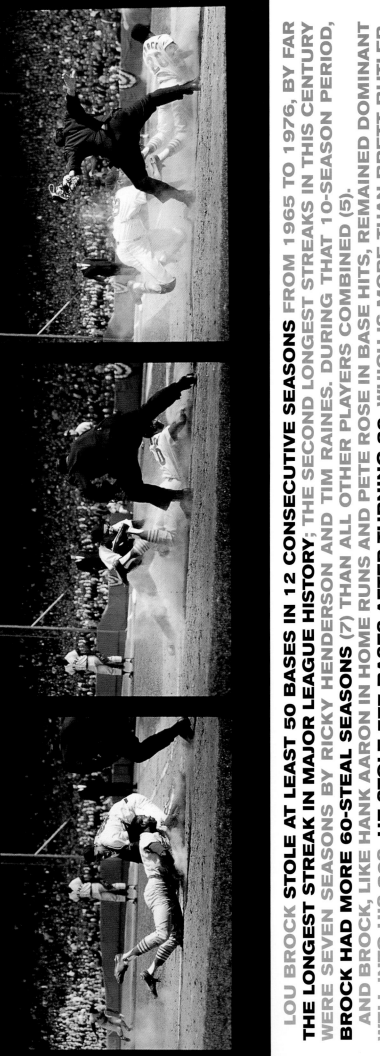

LOU BROCK STOLE AT LEAST 50 BASES IN 12 CONSECUTIVE SEASONS FROM FROM 1965 TO 1976, BY FAR THE LONGEST STREAK IN MAJOR LEAGUE HISTORY; THE SECOND LONGEST STREAKS IN THIS CENTURY WERE SEVEN SEASONS BY RICKY HENDERSON AND TIM RAINES. DURING THAT 10-SEASON PERIOD, BROCK HAD MORE 60-STEAL SEASONS (7) THAN ALL OTHER PLAYERS COMBINED (5).

AND BROCK, LIKE HANK AARON IN HOME RUNS AND PETE ROSE IN BASE HITS, REMAINED DOMINANT WELL INTO HIS 30S. HE STOLE 577 BASES AFTER TURNING 30, WHICH IS MORE THAN BRETT BUTLER, DAVEY LOPES OR LUIS APARICIO STOLE IN THEIR ENTIRE CAREERS.

THOUGH BROCK BECAME ONE OF THE GREAT PLAYERS OF HIS ERA PLAYING FOR THE ST. LOUIS CARDINALS, HE WILL HAVE A PLACE IN CHICAGO CUBS HISTORY FOREVER. BROCK WAS BATTING .251 WITH TWO HOME RUNS IN JUNE OF 1964 WHEN THE CUBS TRADED HIM TO ST. LOUIS. BROCK WOUND UP SECOND IN THE NL IN STOLEN BASES (43) AND FIFTH IN BATTING AVERAGE (.315), HELPING THE CARDINALS STEAL THE CLOSEST THREE-WAY RACE IN BASEBALL HISTORY.

"One time he hit a line drive right past my ear. I turned around and saw the ball hit his ass sliding into second. ★ SATCHEL PAIGE ON JAMES "COOL PAPA" BELL

COOL
PAPA

"In '22, we played the Detroit Tigers. There were only two players who wouldn't play—Ty Cobb and Harry Heilmann. Cobb had played down in Cuba and a black catcher named Petway threw him out stealing 16 times out of 17. After that, he said, he never would play against blacks again. Anyway, we played them and beat them two out of three. After that series, Judge Landis said the major leaguers would have to play us as all-stars and not as an entire team.

When the Western League folded in 1931, most of the players went East. I stole 175 bases out there one year. That was in 1933, my first full season with the Pittsburgh Crawfords."

JAMES "COOL PAPA" BELL
Quoted by John M. Coates, October 1973/Black Sports.

ACCORDING TO LEGEND, COOL PAPA BELL IS SAID TO HAVE ONCE CIRCLED THE BASES AT 12 SECONDS FLAT, AS MUCH AS A SECOND FASTER THAN ANYONE ELSE EVER RECORDED.

"Not even a home run with the bases crammed can quite demoralize an infield and get the defense up in the air as clever base running can do. Such base running strikes deep at the foundation of the defense. It destroys confidence and when confidence is gone, everything is gone. When a fast runner gets to first base and then starts running wild and gets away with it, he completely demoralizes the infield and gets the pitcher and catcher up in the air as well. Infielders get to throwing the ball around, missing plays, making errors and looking like a lot of boobs. They become completely rattled and when a ballplayer is rattled he is done for the time being. He might just as well take off his uniform and go to the clubhouse."

★

TY COBB IN A 1917 INTERVIEW FOR *BASEBALL MAGAZINE*

"I THINK IT'S SMARTER TO SLIDE HEAD FIRST. I WOULD RATHER HAVE AN ARM

"HE DIDN'T JUST COME TO PLAY, HE CAME TO BEAT YOU."

★

LEO DUROCHER ON JACKIE ROBINSON

"SPIKED THAN AN ANKLE — PLUS YOU GET YOUR PICTURE IN THE PAPER."

PETE ROSE ★ 1976

"IT'S NOT HOW FAST YOU ARE, IT'S

"YOU HAVE TO HAVE WILL POWER TO SUCCEED. THAT'S WHAT ALL GREAT PLAYERS HAVE IN COMMON. I'VE SEEN A LOT OF GUYS COME AND GO WHO SAID THEY WOULD LIKE TO STEAL BASES. IT'S NOT ENOUGH TO LIKE TO STEAL BASES. YOU HAVE TO WANT TO STEAL BASES. THERE IS A DIFFERENCE BETWEEN LIKING AND WANTING. THE REASON I FIRST WANTED TO STEAL BASES WAS BECAUSE I HAD A GUIDANCE COUNSELOR AT OAKLAND TECH. SHE GAVE ME A QUARTER OR 50 CENTS EVERY TIME I STOLE A BASE. SHE WAS THE ONE WHO MOTIVATED ME. SHE'S THE ONE I OWE IT ALL TO."

RICKEY HENDERSON

"HOW WELL YOU USE YOUR SPEED."

FIELDING

"THE ONLY WAY TO GET BETTER AT FIELDING A GROUND BALL IS TO DO IT AND DO IT THE RIGHT WAY OVER AND OVER. THERE ARE NO SHORTCUTS IN BASEALL. IF YOU'RE GOING TO BE A PLAYER YOU HAVE TO DO IT OVER AND OVER AND OVER. YOU'RE GOING TO FAIL. THE ONES WHO MAKE IT KEEP AFTER IT."

★ FORMER MAJOR LEAGUE SHORTSTOP **BUCKY DENT**

&THROWING

ROBIN YOUNT   ROBERTO CLEMENTE   HAROLD "PIE" TRAYNOR   AL KALINE   CARLTON FISK

"I remember playing with Roberto Clemente for two years in Puerto Rico. He did things that were amazing. Guys like him were arrogant, but in a good way. They had that swagger. I mean, they just knew they could play. He could go 0-for-16 and you wouldn't know the difference. Those guys work on their weaknesses in batting practice."

DEACON JONES ★ SPECIAL ASSIGNMENT SCOUT FOR THE BALTIMORE ORIOLES

"AFTER STAN MUSIAL, ROBERTO CLEMENTE WAS

THE BEST ALL-AROUND BALLPLAYER I EVER SAW

I PLACED HIM SLIGHTLY ABOVE WILLIE MAYS. AND CLEMENTE COULD THROW. EVEN BETTER THAN MAYS. HE WAS MORE ACCURATE."

HANK SAUER ★ SAN FRANCISCO GIANTS SCOUT AND 1952 NL MVP

"Some nights, even long after games, I'll replay in my mind all the plays I made. I know many of them probably look like they were routine. But sometimes there are tricky ones that no one else sees. The ultimate compliment is to make a tough play look easier, even if no one else notices."

★

CAL RIPKEN

"I WAS BLESSED WITH THE INSTINCT TO BE WHERE THE BALL WAS HIT. I WASN'T FAST AND I DIDN'T HAVE A GREAT ARM, BUT I COMPENSATED BY QUICKLY GETTING MY FEET IN POSITION TO THROW. CONSIDERING THE TOOLS I HAD, I GOT MORE OUT OF MY CAREER THAN I DESERVED."

★ **BROOKS ROBINSON**, WHO WON A RECORD 16 CONSECUTIVE GOLD GLOVES

"DON McMAHON WAS 40 YEARS OLD, PITCHING FOR THE GIANTS. HE LOOKS OUT TO CENTER AND SEES WILLIE MAYS SHADING THE HITTER TO PULL HIM AND HE'S THINKING, 'THIS GUY NEVER HAS PULLED ME IN HIS LIFE.' HE WINDS UP AND THROWS HIM HIS BEST FASTBALL. LINE DRIVE RIGHT AT MAYS. WHEN THE INNING WAS OVER, McMAHON ASKED WILLIE WHY HE WAS PLAYING THE HITTER TO PULL HIM WHEN HE NEVER HAD PULLED HIM IN HIS LIFE. WILLIE TOLD HIM HE COULD SEE FROM CENTER FIELD HE WAS LOSING A LITTLE OFF HIS FASTBALL. WILLIE WOULD STEAL SIGNS STANDING ON FIRST BASE AND HE WOULD STEAL SIGNS STANDING ON SECOND BASE. WILLIE MAYS WAS A BASEBALL INTELLECTUAL, BLESSED WITH MAGNIFICENT TALENT AND EXTREMELY SMART."

FORMER CATCHER FRAN HEALY ★ A METS BROADCASTER, TEAMED WITH WILLIE MAYS ON THE SAN FRANCISCO GIANTS.

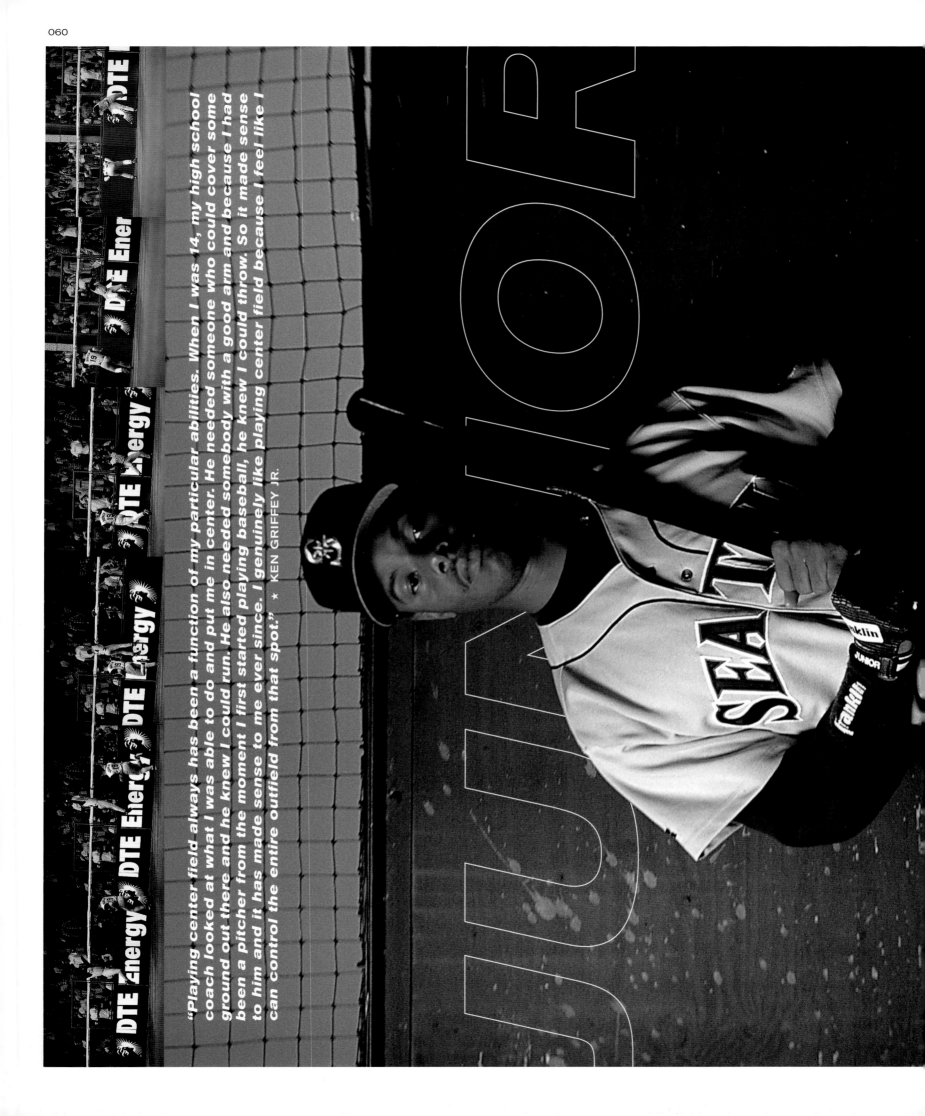

"Playing center field always has been a function of my particular abilities. When I was 14, my high school coach looked at what I was able to do and put me in center. He needed someone who could cover some ground out there and he knew I could run. He also needed somebody with a good arm and because I had been a pitcher from the moment I first started playing baseball, he knew I could throw. So it made sense to him and it has made sense to me ever since. I genuinely like playing center field because I feel like I can control the entire outfield from that spot." ★ KEN GRIFFEY JR.

"WHAT JUNIOR IS GOING TO DO THROUGHOUT THE COURSE OF HIS CAREER IS GOING TO WELL OVERTAKE ANYTHING I'VE EVER DONE. JUNIOR STARTED IN THE GAME THREE YEARS YOUNGER THAN I WAS WHEN I CAME INTO THE LEAGUE. HE IS GOING TO TAKE THE GAME TO ANOTHER LEVEL THAT I DON'T THINK ANYONE IS GOING TO BE ABLE TO CATCH UP TO. SURE, SOMEDAY THERE WILL BE SOME OTHER KID WHO COMES ALONG AND MAY BE AS GOOD AS HIM. BUT **JUNIOR WILL SURPASS ME THROUGHOUT HIS CAREER, BY A LOT. NOT BY A LITTLE. BY A LOT.**"

★

SAN FRANCISCO GIANTS OUTFIELDER
BARRY BONDS

IF JOHNNY BENCH IS THE MOST DOMINANT CATCHER OF THE CENTURY, THEN IVAN RODRIGUEZ IS ONLY RUNNER UP.

On defense alone, Rodriguez quickly is approaching Bench's record 10 Gold Gloves. Through the 1998 season, Rodriguez had eight and he was on pace for No. 9 in 1999. Rodriguez allowed only one stolen base per 24.5 innings during the 1990s, 25 percent fewer than the catcher with the second lowest rate (Charles Johnson, one SB per 18.4 innings). With two weeks left in the 1999 season, opposing runners stole bases exactly the same number of times they were thrown out by Rodriguez (382). To

put that into perspective, no other catcher had a stolen base rate lower than 57 percent with a minimum of 5,000 innings through the 1990s. While it should be noted there were no meaningful records kept on stolen base rates before 1990, it's a good bet no one but Bench threw out as many as often as Rodriguez throughout the 1900s. If Bench's postseason numbers are any indication, he might have thrown out substantially more than 50 percent during his career.

"I THINK JOHNNY BENCH IS THE GREATEST CATCHER EVER TO PLAY THE GAME. I MEAN, I HEAR PEOPLE SAY THAT I HAVE BETTER MECHANICS THAN JOHNNY BENCH, BUT COME ON, TO ME, I'M JUST ANOTHER PLAYER COMPARED TO THAT GUY. HE'S THE BEST. THE VERY BEST."

IVAN RODRIGUEZ

"The thing about Ozzie was his popularity. I had him for 10 years and we played in three World Series during his prime. He got a ton of attention and even when he played, people were saying he was the greatest shortstop who ever lived. Maybe he was. He had a lot of show-manship, a lot of flair for the fans. Fans loved him. He would make diving plays every night. But he was the only player I ever had in St. Louis who got an ovation whenever his name was announced on the road. He was a national hero. He was a lot like George Brett. He also stole bases when they meant something. He was a true team player. He played hurt, he played with aches and pains, he was a guy you could write in that lineup every day and that guy would play."

★

WHITEY HERZOG

065

OZZIE SMITH led all NL shortstops in stolen bases, fielding percentage and assists per game — what might be considered the Speed and Defense Triple Crown — three times (1981, 1984 and 1987). The only other shortstop to lead his league three times was Luis Aparicio (1959 to 1961). Smith also led the NL in assists a record eight times and his career average of 3.3 assists per game ranks second among shortstops during the live-ball era to Hall of Famer Travis Jackson (3.5).

When Smith goes down in baseball annals, he'll be remembered as the greatest defensive shortstop who ever lived, just like Brooks Robinson was the greatest defensive third baseman who ever lived.

"THERE WERE DRILLS I DID WHEN I WAS YOUNG, THINGS I LOOK BACK ON THAT I DIDN'T KNOW AT TIME, BUT THINGS THAT WERE ABLE TO MAKE ME THE PLAYER I WAS. I USED TO LAY DOWN AND THROW THE BALL UP IN THE AIR AND TRY TO CATCH IT WITH MY EYES CLOSED. THAT WAY I WOULD GET THE FEEL OF THE BALL WITHOUT SEEING IT. I WOULD TRY TO GET IT TO HIT THE SAME PART OF MY GLOVE ALL THE TIME. I USED TO ALWAYS THROW THE BALL OFF MY MOM'S STEPS, TOO. SOMETIMES, I WOULD BREAK A FEW WINDOWS DOING IT. MY MOM WOULD YELL, 'BOY, DON'T THROW THE BALL OFF THOSE STEPS.' BUT IT REALLY DEVELOPED MY BACKHAND AND FOREHAND. MY OWN SON DOES IT NOW, THROWING THE BALL OFF THE HOUSE, BUT I REALLY CAN'T GET MAD AT HIM BECAUSE I DID THE SAME THING WHEN I WAS YOUNG. WE HAD A SLANTED ROOF GROWING UP, TOO. I THOUGHT I WAS SO FAST THAT I COULD THROW IT UP ON ONE SIDE AND TRY TO CATCH IT ON THE OTHER. STUPID, HUH? I DON'T THINK I EVER CAUGHT THE BALL, BUT I GOT CLOSE. AND THAT BUILT DETERMINATION AND TENACITY. IT WAS THAT DRIVE THAT HELPED ME IN MY CAREER."

★

OZZIE SMITH

"PITCHERS, LIKE POETS, ARE BORN NOT MADE." ★ **CY YOUNG**

PITCHING

JIM PALMER   BOB FELLER   WHITEY FORD   LEFTY GROVE   STEVE CARLTON

SATCHEL PAIGE'S REPERTOIRE *INCLUDED A VARIETY OF DELIVERIES INCLUDING OVERHAND, SIDEARM AND EVEN SOMETHING APPROXIMATING UNDERHAND. HE ALSO NAMED HIS MOST FAMOUS PITCHES:*

"A BUNCH OF FELLOWS GET IN A BARBER SESSION THE OTHER DAY AND THEY START TO ARGUE ABOUT THE BEST PITCHER THEY EVER SEE. I KNOW WHO'S THE BEST PITCHER I EVER SEE AND IT'S OLD SATCHEL PAIGE. MY FASTBALL LOOKS LIKE A CHANGE OF PACE ALONGSIDE THAT LITTLE PISTOL BULLET OLD SATCHEL SHOOTS UP TO THE PLATE. SATCHEL PAIGE, WITH THOSE LONG ARMS OF HIS, IS MY IDEA OF THE PITCHER WITH THE GREATEST STUFF I EVER SAW."

DIZZY DEAN ★ 1969

1

THE BARBER
A rising fastball that rode up
under a batter's chin

2

LITTLE TOM
A medium fastball

3

LONG TOM
The fastball

4

HESITATION PITCH
Paige would stop in the middle of his windup
before continuing to throw to the plate

5

TWO-HUMP BLOOPER
An extremely slow pitch
that tended to move decidedly

"The bigger the major league stars, the more Paige bore down. According to eye-witness accounts, he struck out Rogers Hornsby five time in one game, Charley Gehringer three times in another, Jimmie Foxx three times in a third. In 1934, in Hollywood, Paige pitched what Bill Veeck said is the greatest game he ever saw. In that game, which lasted 13 innings, Paige was opposed by Dizzy Dean, a 30-game winner for the Cardinals. Dean was superlative, holding the Paige Stars to one run and fanning 15. But Paige shut out the Dean Stars and fanned 17. After the game, Dean informed the press that Paige was the best pitcher in the business (1934). In three previous winters in California the Paige Stars had won 128 games, at least 40 of them against teams of major league stars, while losing 23."

RICHARD DONOVAN ★ Collier's Magazine, 1953

"STEVE CARLTON
DOES NOT PITCH TO THE HITTER, HE PITCHES THROUGH HIM. THE BATTER HARDLY EXISTS FOR STEVE. HE'S PLAYING AN ELEVATED GAME OF CATCH."

TIM McCARVER ★ FORMER PHILADELPHIA PHILLIES CATCHER, 1980

46%
OF TEAM VICTORIES IN 1972

When Steve Carlton posted a 27-10 record in 1972 for the Phillies, it was by far the most victories this century for a pitcher on a team with the worst record in its league. Carlton had an amazing 46 percent of the team's victories, the highest percentage during the 1900s. No other Philadelphia pitcher won more than four starts. Carlton also ranks second in career strikeouts (4,136), a significant feat because no other left-hander ranks among the top 12.

"HE'S SO GOOD THAT BLIND PEOPLE COME TO THE PARK JUST TO HEAR HIM PITCH."

★

REGGIE JACKSON ON TOM SEAVER, 1969.

TOM SEAVER struck out at least 200 batters in nine consecutive seasons from 1968 to 1976, the longest streak in major league history. Seaver also led the National League in victories in three different decades (1969, 1975 and 1981) — another of those accidents of timing, but only two other pitchers did so in their respective leagues: Bob Feller and Warren Spahn. Despite his greatness, Seaver won 311 games to rank 16th on the all-time list, there was an enormous difference in his career record in odd-numbered years (178-88, .669) and even-numbered years (133-117, .532).

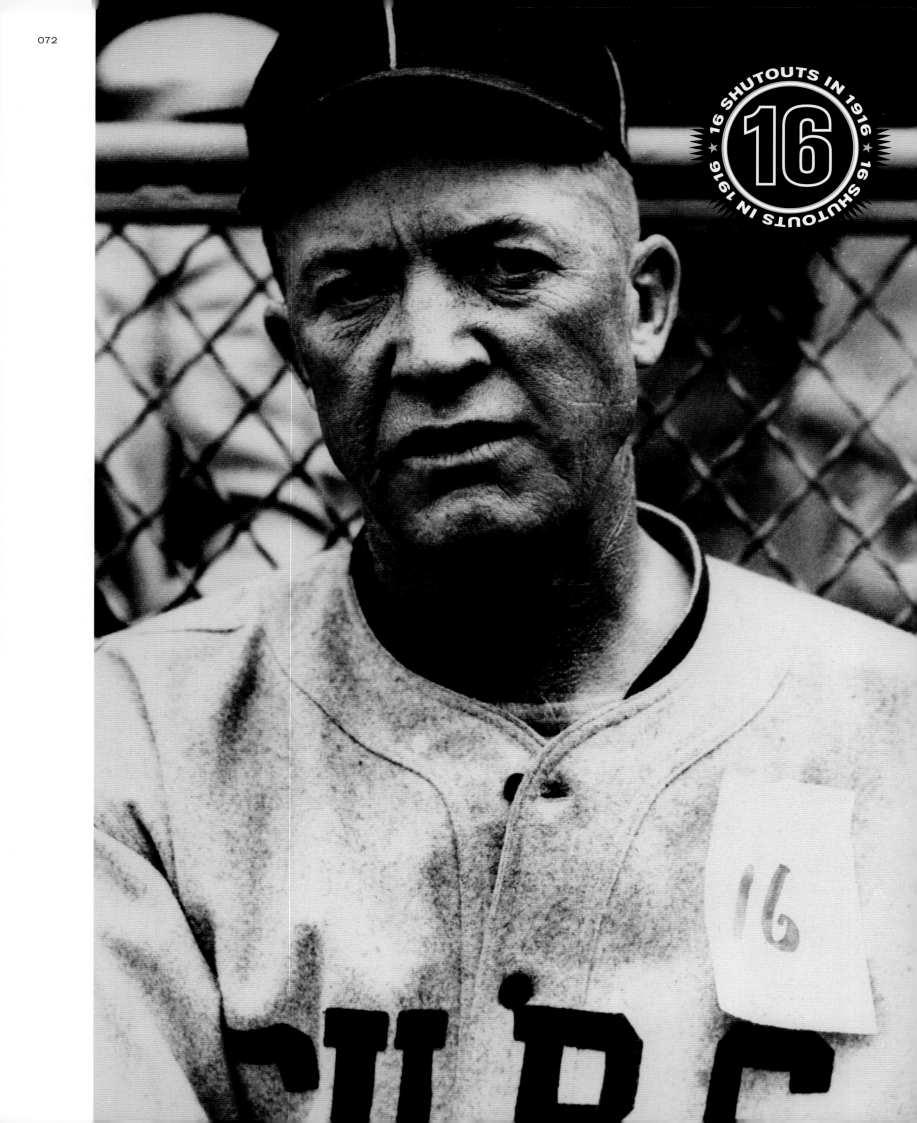

16 SHUTOUTS IN 1916 ★ 16 SHUTOUTS IN 1916

★ **JUST AS CY YOUNG'S CAREER WAS DIVIDED EVENLY BETWEEN THE 19TH AND 20TH CENTURIES, GROVER CLEVELAND ALEXANDER'S WAS SPLIT BETWEEN THE DEAD- AND LIVE-BALL ERAS.**

The differences that occurred over Alexander's career were enormous, owing mainly to the introduction of the live-ball. In 1911, there were 514 home runs hit in the entire majors. In 1930, the top 15 home-run hitters produced more homers than the entire majors did in 1911.

Still, Alexander thrived in both environments. He won 208 games from 1911 to 1919, when he was at his best. He led the majors with 28 wins in 1911 and is the only rookie to have done so in the 20th century. He led the majors in victories in three consecutive seasons from 1915 to 1917, a feat matched or exceeded only twice since, by Hal Newhouser (1944-1946) and Robin Roberts (1952-1955). Alexander missed most of the 1918 season in military service, from which he returned suffering from deafness in one ear and epilepsy. Although he never reached the heights in the 1920s that he had in the previous decade, his total of 165 wins during the '20s ranked third in the majors behind a pair of Hall of Famers: Burleigh Grimes (190) and Eppa Rixey (166). Only one pitcher other than Alexander earned even 100 wins in both the dead- and live-ball eras: Walter Johnson (297 and 120, respectively).

Within a career of superlatives, Alexander has three signature achievements. He shares with Christy Mathewson the all-time National League record for career wins (373). He shares with George Bradley the record for shutouts in a season (16). And he made a legendary relief appearance to save Game 7 of the 1926 World Series. All are noteworthy for reasons that go beyond the feats themselves.

Alexander pitched 16 shutouts in 1916 tying the record set by Bradley in 1876,

THE FACT THAT ALEXANDER WAS ONE OF THE GAME'S BEST PITCHERS THROUGHOUT HIS CAREER, REGARDLESS OF THE CHANGING RULES AND CONDITIONS, WAS EXTRAORDINARY.

the National League's first season (when the league ERA was a paltry 2.31). The total alone is impressive — three more than Bob Gibson had in his remarkable 1968 season. But it's all the more outstanding because Alexander pitched his home games in Baker Bowl, the second-best hitters' park in the National League at that time. Baker Bowl increased scoring by about 8 percent, but Alexander pitched nine of his 16 shutouts there in 1916.

Alexander's performance for the Cardinals in the 1926 World Series is worthy of the legend it quickly became. Alexander not only struck out second baseman Tony Lazzeri with the bases loaded to choke off a Yankees rally in the seventh inning of the seventh game, but he did so after pitching a complete game victory the day before in Game 6. To earn St. Louis its first World Series championship, Alexander had to preserve a one-run lead for two more innings after throwing nine innings the previous day.

This also suggests that the story that Alexander was badly hungover from celebrating his Game 6 victory is seriously overstated, if not an outright fabrication. Manager Rogers Hornsby would hardly have asked Alexander to go that long — with a one-run lead, against the dangerous Yankees lineup without a day of rest — if he was as shaky as the legend would have us believe. Then again…

"I looked into his eyes and saw that they were bloodshot, but they weren't foggy," said Hornsby when asked why he turned to Alexander. "I gave him the ball and told him to get Lazzeri."

ALEXANDER
1911 TO 1917

YEAR	VICTORIES	
★ 1911	28	LED THE MAJORS
1912	19	
1913	22	
1914	27	
1915	31	LED THE MAJORS FOR THREE CONSECUTIVE YEARS
1916	33	
1917	30	

★ ⟶ ALEXANDER'S ROOKIE YEAR. THE ONLY ROOKIE TO HAVE DONE SO IN THE 20TH CENTURY.

"I'M NOT SO SURE IT WAS THAT HE WANTED TO WIN SO BADLY OR HE JUST HATED TO LOSE."

"ONE GAME COMES TO MIND WHEN I THINK OF BOB. IT WAS 1965 IN MY SECOND ALL-STAR GAME AND I HAD CAUGHT THE WHOLE GAME. IT WAS THE NINTH INNING AND THE NATIONAL LEAGUE HAD A 6-5 LEAD. TONY OLIVA WAS THE HITTER. NOW BEFORE THE GAME, BOB

NEVER SAID ANYTHING. WE GET STRIKE ONE, THEN STRIKE TWO ON OLIVA. I DEBATED WITH MYSELF AS TO WHETHER I SHOULD GO OUT TO THE MOUND AND TALK WITH HIM. I WANTED THE NEXT PITCH TO BE A FASTBALL UP AND IN. I DIDN'T WANT THE PITCH COMING DOWN AND IN BECAUSE OLIVA COULD HANDLE THAT. I THOUGHT, 'I'LL SECOND GUESS MYSELF IF I DON'T TALK TO HIM AND SOMETHING HAPPENS.' SO I WENT OUT TO THE MOUND. BOB LOOKED AT ME LIKE I WASN'T EVEN THERE, NEVER ACKNOW- LEDGED MY PRESENCE. HE THREW A FASTBALL DOWN AND IN AND OLIVA HIT A DOUBLE TO LEFT-CENTER FIELD. IT WAS AS IF NOTHING HAD HAPPENED. BOB GETS THE NEXT GUY TO POP OUT AND THEN STRIKES OUT THE NEXT TWO AND WE WIN THE GAME. I SAW BOB IN THE SHOWER AND CONGRATU- LATED HIM. REMEMBER, WE WEREN'T TEAMMATES YET. I WAS PLAYING FOR THE BRAVES AND BOB WAS WITH THE CARDINALS. HE NEVER ACKNOWLEDGED ME. DIDN'T SAY A WORD. JUST LOOKED STRAIGHT AHEAD AND SOAPED HIMSELF UP. HE'S A REMARKABLE INDIVIDUAL. ONCE YOU GET PAST THAT GRUFF EXTERIOR THERE'S A WARM, CARING PERSON. IT DIDN'T TAKE ME LONG TO GET TO THAT PERSON ONCE I GOT TRADED OVER TO THE CARDINALS."

★

NEW YORK YANKEES MANAGER
JOE TORRE WAS A NINE-TIME ALL STAR

> "THE ONE WORD TO USE WITH ROGER CLEMENS
> IS THE ONE WORD YOU USED
> WITH BOB GIBSON, AND THAT IS 'WAR.'"
>
> ★
> JOE TORRE

"I WAS IN MY FIRST YEAR AS SCOUTING DIRECTOR OF THE METS. WE HAD TAKEN ROGER CLEMENS IN THE 12TH ROUND AFTER HE SPENT A YEAR AT A JUNIOR COLLEGE. HARRY MINOR WENT DOWN AND SAW HIM PITCH ONCE AND SAID HE WAS WORTH A $15,000 BONUS. CLEMENS INSISTED ON $25,000. WE HAD JUST HIRED THE AREA SCOUT, JIM TERRELL, AND WE WEREN'T SURE HOW GOOD HIS JUDGMENT WAS. HE KEPT INSISTING I COME LOOK AT CLEMENS MYSELF. I SPENT TWO WEEKENDS IN HOUSTON. IT RAINED ALL WEEKEND BOTH TIMES AND I NEVER DID GET TO SEE HIM PITCH. ALL I DID WAS TALK TO HIM IN THE PARKING LOT TO TRY TO CONVINCE HIM TO SIGN. WHEN THAT HAPPENS, YOU JUST HAVE TO SAY SOMETIMES THINGS JUST AREN'T MEANT TO BE. SOME HIGHER POWER HAD OTHER IDEAS THAN FOR ROGER CLEMENS TO PITCH IN NEW YORK. WE WOULD HAVE HAD DOC GOODEN AND ROGER CLEMENS IN THEIR PRIME AT THE SAME TIME. OH WELL."

JOE MCILVAINE ★ FORMER METS GENERAL MANAGER, SCOUT FOR THE MINNESOTA TWINS

WHAT WOULD THE REQUIREMENTS BE FOR A PITCHE

FIRST, HE WOULD HAVE TO WIN MORE GAMES AND ALLOW FEWER RUNS THAN ANY PITCHER OF HIS GENERATION AND DO SO BY A WIDE MARGIN. SECOND, HE WOULD HAVE TO BE CONSISTENT OVER AN EXTENDED PERIOD OF TIME. BASED ON THAT CRITERIA THERE ARE TWO PITCHERS WHO STAND ABOVE THE REST DURING THE 20TH CENTURY: DURING THE DEAD-BALL ERA, WALTER JOHNSON; DURING THE LIVE-BALL ERA, **GREG MADDUX.**

TO BE CONSIDERED *THE GREATEST OF THE CENTURY?*

With two weeks remaining in the 1999 season, Maddux already was assured of leading the majors in victories during the 1990s, and of doing so by a wide margin. Maddux's total of 175 victories was nearly 10 percent more than his nearest rival, longtime teammate Tom Glavine (161). No one else had more than 151 victories, not even the pair of pitchers who rank third and fourth, and who are regarded widely as Cooperstown contenders based in large part on what they accomplished during the '90s, Roger Clemens (151) and Randy Johnson (147).

Maddux has ranked in the National League's top 10 in victories in every season since 1988. That 12-season streak ties Christy Mathewson for the third longest in major league history, trailing only those of Warren Spahn (17) and Cy Young (14).

Besides winning games at a rate to be expected of a "greatest pitcher ever", Maddux has posted ERAs that are unprecedented during the live-ball era when judged in relation to league figures.

During the seven years from 1992 through 1998, the National League ERA was 4.08; each season contributed to the average in proportion to the number of innings Maddux pitched. Maddux's ERA was 2.15, which is 47.2 percent lower than the NL mark. That's the largest such gap in major league history over a span as long as seven years. Only one pitcher was even close. Using unofficial figures for the first two years of the period, Walter Johnson's 1.55 ERA from 1910 through 1916 was 47.1 percent lower than the AL average (2.94). The following table lists the five largest gaps, using unofficial published totals for ERAs before to 1912. (Note: Differences and percentages are calculated exactly then rounded, so that they may appear fractionally incorrect):

7-YR. SPAN	PITCHER	ERA	LEAGUE	DIFF.	PCT.
1992-1998	GREG MADDUX	2.15	4.08	1.92	47.2%
1910-1916	WALTER JOHNSON	1.55	2.94	1.38	47.1%
1904-1910	MORDECAI BROWN	1.56	2.68	1.11	41.5%
1926-1932	LEFTY GROVE	2.64	4.28	1.64	38.4%
1906-1912	ED WALSH	1.71	2.76	1.05	38.1%

It's noteworthy that even if different timespans are used, Maddux and Johnson invariably place first and second (though not always in that order). That was true for every span all the way from two years — based on Maddux's outstanding 1994 and 1995 seasons, and Johnson's 1912 and 1913 — to 11 years. It was true even over four years, which allowed Sandy Koufax to be measured on the terms most favorable to him — that is, his great period from 1963 to 1966. The following table shows how Maddux and Johnson bested Koufax even on Sandy's own terms:

4-YR. SPAN	PITCHER	ERA	LEAGUE	DIFF.	PCT.
1910-1913	WALTER JOHNSON	1.42	3.02	1.60	52.9%
1994-1997	GREG MADDUX	2.06	4.20	2.14	50.9%
1906-1909	MORDECAI BROWN	1.31	2.51	1.20	48.0%
1963-1966	SANDY KOUFAX	1.86	3.49	1.64	46.8%
1928-1931	LEFTY GROVE	2.49	4.33	1.84	42.6%

Those are measures of extreme excellence, good for separating the great from the good.

Maddux's greatness has all the other trimmings one would expect: four Cy Young awards, four ERA titles and seven All-Star nominations. He also has one you wouldn't expect: nine Gold Gloves. Still, history doesn't always reveal itself in real time. It's often left to later generations to identify greatness in hindsight.

That might be particularly true in Maddux's case. Today's pitchers are at a great disadvantage when their statistics are compared to those of pitchers from the past without compensating for the changes that have taken place.

Compared to the huge victory totals of the 1920s or the 1970s, or the tiny ERAs of the 1960s or the dead-ball era, Maddux's numbers aren't exceptional. So the suggestion that today's fans might be watching the greatest pitcher of the century, if not of all time, may seem unexpected, overstated, or even blasphemous. A closer look at Maddux's record, and an understanding of the times in which he pitches, indicate that it is none of the above. He just might be the best ever.

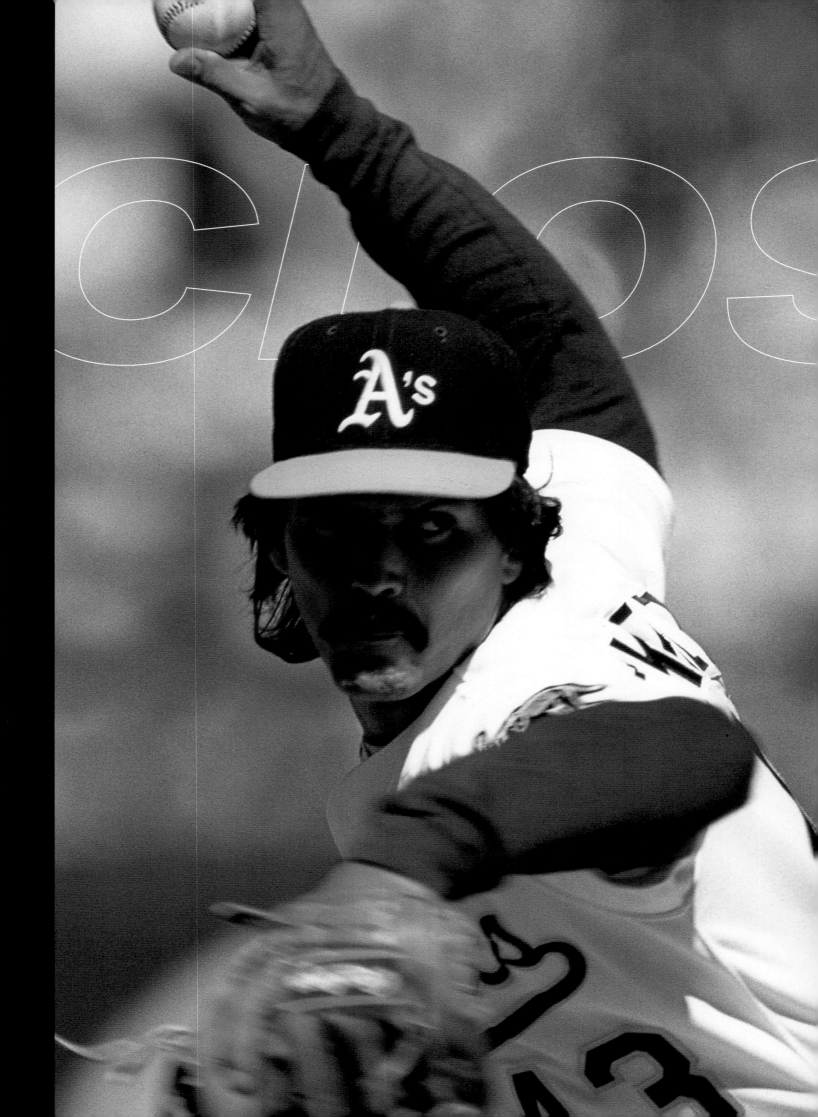

"He has always been a warrior. On the mound. Always. When he was young and crazy. When he was in Oakland, winning the Cy Young and MVP. And (when) I saw him in his 40s, it was still the same. I've never seen him take the mound and not be ready for the competition. The fire in his belly was just the way it was when he was a rookie."

TONY LARUSSA MANAGED DENNIS ECKERSLEY IN ST. LOUIS AND OAKLAND

SERS

"Being an idiot helps if you are a closer, especially in this town. When you don't get the job done, something is wrong with you. When you do get the job done, well it's only one inning, you're supposed to do it. You have to be an idiot to want a job like that. But you also have to have a certain mental toughness. You can't think about a bad one when you just have to turn the page. I don't think that is something you can develop. It's something inside you!"

NEW YORK METS CLOSER JOHN FRANCO, SECOND TO LEE SMITH ON THE ALL-TIME SAVES LIST

BOB GIBSON WALTER JOHNSON SANDY KOUFAX CHRISTY MATHEWS
ERNIE BANKS CAL RIPKEN JR. MARK MCGWIRE HONUS WAGNER
TY COBB JOE DIMAGGIO KEN GRIFFEY JR.
PETE ROSE BABE RUTH
ROGER CLEMENS
CHRISTY MATHEWSON NOLAN RYAN WARREN SPAHN
ROGERS HORNSBY HANK
BROOKS ROBINSON MIKE SCHMIDT
MICKEY MANTLE WILL
TED WILLIAMS JOHNNY BENCH YOGI BERRA
LEFTY GROVE BOB GIBSON WALTER JOHNSON
CY YOUNG LOU GEHRIG
SANDY KOUFAX JACKIE ROBINSON ERNIE BANKS CAL RIPKEN JR.
HANK AARON TY COBB JOE DIMAGGIO
WILLIE MAYS STAN MUSIAL PETE ROSE BABE RUTH
GI BERRA
HNSON SANDY KOUFAX CHRISTY MATHEWSON
MARK MCGWIRE
L RIPKEN JR. HONUS WAGNER BROOKS ROBINSON
JOE DIMAGGIO KEN GRIFFEY JR. TED WILLIAMS JOHNNY BENCH
ROGER CLEMENS LEFTY GROVE
NOLAN RYAN WARREN SPAHN CY YOUNG LOU GEHRIG
ROGERS HORNSBY JACKIE ROBINSON
BROOKS ROBINSON MIKE SCHMIDT HANK AARON
MICKEY MANTLE WILLIE

ALL CENT

★ **THE ALL-CENTURY TEAM CONSISTS OF 30 PLAYERS, 25 OF WHOM WERE SELECTED THROUGH A NATIONAL VOTING PROGRAM THAT CONCLUDE**

JOHNNY BENCH ROY CAMPANELLA MICKEY COCHRANE YOGI BERRA BILL DICKEY CARLTON FISK JOSH GIBSON GABBY HARTNE
FINGERS WHITEY FORD BOB GIBSON CARL HUBBELL WALTER JOHNSON GREG MADDUX SANDY KOUFAX JUAN MARICHAL CHRISTY MAT
J GEHRIG HANK GREENBERG HARMON KILLEBREW BUCK LEONARD WILLIE MCCOVEY MARK MCGWIRE EDDIE MURRAY GEORGE SISLER
N LUIS APARICIO LUKE APPLING ERNIE BANKS JOE CRONIN CAL RIPKEN JR. OZZIE SMITH HONUS WAGNER ROBIN YOUNT GEORGE BRE
CAR CHARLESTON ROBERTO CLEMENTE TY COBB GOOSE GOSLIN JOE DIMAGGIO TONY GWYNN KEN GRIFFEY JR. HARRY HEILMANN RICH
TH FRANK ROBINSON PETE ROSE AL SIMMONS BABE RUTH DUKE SNIDER TRIS SPEAKER WILLIE STARGELL PAUL WANER BILLY WILL
L GABBY HARTNETT GROVER C ALEXANDER MORDECAI BROWN STEVE CARLTON ROGER CLEMENS DIZZY DEAN DENNIS ECKERSLEY
RICHAL CHRISTY MATHEWSON SATCHEL PAIGE JIM PALMER EDDIE PLANK ROBIN ROBERTS NOLAN RYAN TOM SEAVER WARREN SPAHN
FRAY GEORGE SISLER BILL TERRY ROD CAREW EDDIE COLLINS FRANKIE FRISCH CHARLIE GEHRINGER ROGERS HORNSBY NAPOLEO
BIN YOUNT GEORGE BRETT EDDIE MATHEWS PAUL MOLITOR BROOKS ROBINSON PIE TRAYNOR MIKE SCHMIDT COOL PAPA BELL HANK
HARRY HEILMANN RICKEY HENDERSON JOE JACKSON REGGIE JACKSON AL KALINE WILLIE KEELER RALPH KINER WILL
L WANER BILLY WILLIAMS TED WILLIAMS CARL YASTRZEMSKI JOHNNY BENCH ROY CAMPANELLA MICKEY COCHRANE YOGI BERRA
NNIS ECKERSLEY BOB FELLER LEFTY GROVE ROLLIE FINGERS WHITEY FORD BOB GIBSON CARL HUBBELL WALTER JOHNSON GREG
RREN SPAHN ED WALSH CY YOUNG JIMMIE FOXX LOU GEHRIG HANK GREENBERG HARMON KILLEBREW BUCK LEONARD WILLIE
RNSBY NAPOLEON LAJOIE JOE MORGAN JACKIE ROBINSON LUIS APARICIO LUKE APPLING ERNIE BANKS JOE CRONIN CAL RIPKEN JR.
PA BELL HANK AARON BARRY BONDS LOU BROCK OSCAR CHARLESTON ROBERTO CLEMENTE TY COBB GOOSE GOSLIN JOE DIMAGGIO
PH KINER WILLIE MAYS JOE MEDWICK STAN MUSIAL MEL OTT FRANK ROBINSON PETE ROSE AL SIMMONS BABE RUTH DUKE SNIDER TR
GI BERRA BILL DICKEY CARLTON FISK JOSH GIBSON GABBY HARTNETT GROVER C ALEXANDER MORDECAI BROWN STEVE CARLTON
HNSON GREG MADDUX SANDY KOUFAX JUAN MARICHAL CHRISTY MATHEWSON SATCHEL PAIGE JIM PALMER EDDIE PLANK ROBIN ROB
L RIPKEN JR. OZZIE SMITH HONUS WAGNER ROBIN YOUNT GEORGE BRETT EDDIE MATHEWS PAUL MOLITOR BROOKS ROBINSON
SLIN JOE DIMAGGIO TONY GWYNN KEN GRIFFEY JR. HARRY HEILMANN RICKEY HENDERSON JOE JACKSON REGGIE JACKSON AL KALINE
TH DUKE SNIDER TRIS SPEAKER WILLIE STARGELL PAUL WANER BILLY WILLIAMS TED WILLIAMS CARL YASTRZEMSKI JOHNNY BENCH
OWN STEVE CARLTON ROGER CLEMENS DIZZY DEAN DENNIS ECKERSLEY BOB FELLER LEFTY GROVE ROLLIE FINGERS WHITEY FORD
DIE PLANK ROBIN ROBERTS NOLAN RYAN TOM SEAVER WARREN SPAHN ED WALSH CY YOUNG JIMMIE FOXX LOU GEHRIG HANK GRE
LINS FRANKIE FRISCH CHARLIE GEHRINGER ROGERS HORNSBY NAPOLEON LAJOIE JOE MORGAN JACKIE ROBINSON LUIS APARICIO LU
BROOKS ROBINSON PIE TRAYNOR MIKE SCHMIDT HANK AARON BARRY BONDS LOU BROCK OSCAR CHARLESTON R
GGIE JACKSON AL KALINE WILLIE KEELER MICKEY MANTLE RALPH KINER WILLIE MAYS JOE MEDWICK STAN MUSIAL MEL OTT FRANK ROB
ZEMSKI JOHNNY BENCH ROY CAMPANELLA MICKEY COCHRANE YOGI BERRA BILL DICKEY CARLTON FISK JOSH GIBSON GABBY HARTNE
FINGERS WHITEY FORD BOB GIBSON CARL HUBBELL WALTER JOHNSON GREG MADDUX SANDY KOUFAX JUAN MARICHAL CHRISTY MAT
J GEHRIG HANK GREENBERG HARMON KILLEBREW BUCK LEONARD WILLIE MCCOVEY MARK MCGWIRE EDDIE MURRAY GEORGE SISLER
LIS APARICIO LUKE APPLING ERNIE BANKS JOE CRONIN CAL RIPKEN JR. OZZIE SMITH HONUS WAGNER ROBIN YOUNT GEORGE
ROBERTO CLEMENTE TY COBB GOOSE GOSLIN JOE DIMAGGIO KEN GRIFFEY JR.

JRY TEAM

SEPTEMBER 15, 1999. THE ADDITIONAL FIVE PLAYERS WERE SELECTED BY A PANEL OF 22 BASEBALL WRITERS, OFFICIALS AND BROADCASTERS. ★

★

BENCH, JOHNNY [1967–1983]
BERRA, YOGI [1946–1965]
CAMPANELLA, ROY [1948–1957]
COCHRANE, MICKEY [1925–1937]
DICKEY, BILL [1928–1946]
FISK, CARLTON [1969–1993]
GIBSON, JOSH [1930–1946]
HARTNETT, GABBY [1922–1941]

★

CATCHER

ALL-CENTURY TEAM CATCHER ★ ALL-CENTURY TEAM CATCHER ★ ALL-CENTURY TEAM CATCHER ★ ALL-CENTURY TEAM CATCHER ★

JOHNNY BENCH

THE MOST FEARED HITTER ON THE BEST TEAM OF THE 70s

T o a baseball fan of that era, *That '70s Show* would have been the nightly performance at Riverfront Stadium in downtown Cincinnati. With the most powerful attack in baseball, the Reds were guided by their brash young manager to six playoff appearances in 10 years, reaching the World Series four times and winning it twice.

From 1970 to 1979, the Reds posted a winning percentage of .592, the highest by any team since the legendary Yankees of the 1950s. The Reds' offense was so outstanding that their average of 4.68 runs per game during that time was only fractionally lower than that of the Boston Red Sox, who topped the majors at 4.70 with a designated hitter batting in place of their pitchers for most of the decade. In fact, since the Reds led the majors in scoring in both 1975 and 1976, only one National League team has done so (the New York Mets in 1990).

Sparky Anderson's auspicious arrival in 1970 coincided with the start of Cincinnati's rise. He became the only manager in the 1900s to win 70 of his first 100 games. The addition of Joe Morgan in 1972, after the team's disappointing fourth-place finish in 1971, is widely considered the final piece of the puzzle. But the most feared hitter on the best team of the decade was Johnny Bench, who led the team in home runs (290) and RBIs (1,013) during the '70s, and matched Morgan's pair of MVP awards with two of his own.

And just as Morgan gave the Reds the advantage of a second baseman who could produce offensively — unusual in that era — Bench gave his team production unprecedented for a catcher.

Contemporary baseball fans have seen Bench's record for catchers career home runs surpassed by Carlton Fisk. In the last decade, Roy Campanella's longstanding single-season mark was challenged almost annually by Mike Piazza and then broken by Todd Hundley. So it may be surprising to learn only one catcher in major league history led the majors in home runs or RBIs. That was Bench, who led twice in homers (1970 and 1972) and three times in RBIs (1970, 1972, and 1974).

PLAYER	BORN	BIRTHPLACE	BATS	THROWS	HEIGHT	WEIGHT	MAJOR LEAGUE DEBUT
JOHNNY BENCH	12/07/47	OKLAHOMA CITY, OK	R	R	6'1"	208	08/28/67

The following table summarizes the primary positions of each season's major league leaders in home runs and RBIs during the live-ball era. Few baseball fans would be surprised to learn the only second baseman to lead the majors in either category was Rogers Hornsby; or that the only shortstop to lead in homers was Ernie Banks. But who would have thought Bench, no matter how great a hitter, has accomplished something never done by Piazza, Fisk, Campanella, Ivan Rodriguez, Gary Carter, Lance Parrish, Ted Simmons, Thurman Munson, Joe Torre, Yogi Berra, Walker Cooper, Bill Dickey, Mickey Cochrane, Gabby Hartnett, or any of more than 1,000 other players to catch in the majors during that period?

POSITION	C	1B	2B	3B	SS	LF	CF	RF	DH
HOME RUNS	2	23	2	10	2	22	10	19	0
RUNS BATTED IN	3	23	1	6	4	19	8	19	1

Bench was so dominant, not only at his position but in the majors in general, that from 1969 to 1977 he was the only player to start all nine All-Star Games. The only other players to start even half the games during that time were Rod Carew (8) and Hank Aaron, Reggie Jackson and Joe Morgan (6 each).

Bench was recognized widely as the best defensive catcher of his era as well. It's not often that a "freak-show" statistic serves to illustrate a significant point, but this one does: In 45 postseason games, Bench stole as many bases in far fewer attempts (6-for-8) than all opposing players stole while he was catching (6-for-21). From 1970 through 1976, before he began to experience the arm problems that eventually prompted him to move to third base, his record was even greater: Opposing runners stole just two bases in 17 postseason attempts against him.

The fact that no catcher other than Bench ever led the majors in home runs or RBIs speaks loudly of the importance of strong defense at that position. The tougher and more important the position, the less need for offensive contribution. And on that basis, the table shows catchers to rank with the middle infield positions in terms of the importance of defense. Had Bench been merely an adequate offensive player, defense alone might have made him a perennial All-Star. As one of the top offensive players of his era at any position, and perhaps the greatest offensive catcher of the pre-Piazza era, his position on the All-Century Team was assured.

W hen baseball fans speak of the "Yankees dynasty," they refer to a period of 44 years from 1921 to 1964, during which the team played in 29 World Series and won 20 of them.

During those four-plus decades, there were periods of relative strength and relative weakness. For instance, the Yankees made only one trip to the World Series from 1929 to 1935; then went 7-for-8 from 1936 to 1943, before another three-year span without an appearance in the Series. But even within the dynasty, the period from 1947 to 1964 was spectacular: 15 World Series appearances and 10 championships in 18 years. This period coincided exactly with Yogi Berra's contribution to the Yankees, first as a player, then his first tenure as the team's manager.

Records are broken when conditions are ripe. The truly unbreakable records are the ones that would require conditions we're unlikely to see again. With an expanding roster of 30 teams, it's hard to imagine any team reaching the World Series as often over the course of one player's career as did the Yankees during Yogi's career. And so, his record of playing in 75 Series games has as good a chance as any of standing forever.

The top seven in World Series appearances played only for the Yankees: Berra, 75 games; Mickey Mantle, 65; Elston Howard, 54; Hank Bauer and Gil McDougald, 53; Phil Rizzuto, 52; and Joe DiMaggio, 51. To put those totals in perspective, the highest-ranked active player is David Justice, with 26 games through 1998. Although he has played for great teams throughout his career, Justice would have to play every game of seven more World Series — and each would have to go to a seventh game — just to catch Berra. By the way, Berra's record could have been higher: He played in only seven of the Yankees' 16 World Series games from 1961 to 1963.

To link Berra's arrival simplistically to the start of the "dynasty within a dynasty," and his departure to its end, would overlook the contributions of other key players. Whitey Ford arrived in 1950, Mickey Mantle in 1951, Elston Howard in 1955, Roger Maris in 1960 and so on. Casey Stengel replaced Bucky Harris as manager in 1949, the first of five straight championship seasons. Berra was a key member of a great team. But on that team, great as it was, it's just as easy to overlook Berra's contributions.

WORLD SERIES GAME
75
APPEARANCES

HANK BAUER AND GIL MCDOUGALD 53 * PHIL RIZZUTO 52 * JOE DIMAGGIO 51 * MICKEY MANTLE 65 * ELSTON HOWARD 54

FROM 1947 TO 1964

15 | 10

WORLD SERIES | CHAMPIONSHIPS

PLAYER	BORN	BIRTHPLACE	BATS	THROWS	HEIGHT	WEIGHT	MAJOR LEAGUE DEBUT
YOGI BERRA	05/12/25	ST. LOUIS, MO	L	R	5'8"	194	09/22/46

BERRA LED ALL CATCHERS IN BOTH HOME RUNS AND RBIs
IN EACH OF NINE CONSECUTIVE SEASONS FROM 1949 THROUGH 1957
AND HE DID SO BY WIDE MARGINS.

Berra was the dominant hitting catcher in the American League at a time when there was no close number two. He gave the Yankees an extra weapon that no rival team had, as second baseman Joe Morgan did for the Reds a quarter-century later — and as no catcher, not even Morgan's teammate Johnny Bench, has done since. Several NL catchers of Berra's era were productive hitters: Roy Campanella particularly so, Walker Cooper and Andy Seminick to a lesser degree. But until the late '50s, when his brief understudy Gus Triandos developed into a power threat for the Orioles, Berra was the only AL catcher to post strong offensive numbers year in and year out.

Berra led AL catchers in both home runs and RBIs in each of nine consecutive seasons from 1949 through 1957 and he did so by wide margins. His totals for those nine seasons were 235 home runs, 929 RBIs. The totals of each season's runner-up — that is, a composite of the second-highest ranked AL catcher in each category each year — were 131 HRs, 578 RBIs. When Triandos came within five homers and 10 RBIs of Berra's totals in 1957, it marked the first time in nine years that any AL catcher had come that close to Berra in either category. Berra's margin over the runner-up catcher was more than 40 RBIs for six consecutive seasons (1950-1955). And one more thing: He led AL catchers in batting average four times in those nine seasons, ranked second three times and third once. Unreal.

Berra is one of only four players with 100 RBIs in each of four consecutive seasons in which they caught at least 100 games. (The others: Johnny Bench, Bill Dickey and Mike Piazza.) He had only 415 career strikeouts compared to 358 home runs, the third-best ratio in major league history (minimum: 100 HR), behind Joe DiMaggio (361 HR, 369 SO) and Lefty O'Doul (113 HR, 122 SO).

ENTIRE BOOKS AND MAGAZINE ARTICLES HAVE BEEN WRITTEN ABOUT YOGI BERRA'S UNIQUE CONTRIBUTIONS TO THE LANGUAGE. SOME EVEN HAVE BECOME PART OF OUR CULTURE.

"IT'S DEJA VU ALL OVER AGAIN,"

AND "IT AIN'T OVER 'TIL IT'S OVER" ARE USED BY ENGLISH SPEAKERS, MANY OF WHOM WOULDN'T KNOW WHAT TEAM YOGI BERRA PLAYED FOR OR WHAT POSITION HE PLAYED IF INDEED THEY EVEN KNEW HIS NAME. SO HIS ELECTION TO THE ALL CENTURY TEAM IS A REFRESHING OPPORTUNITY TO REVIEW THE ACCOMPLISHMENTS THAT "MADE THIS DAY NECESSARY."

★

APARICIO, LUIS [1956 – 1973]
APPLING, LUKE [1930 – 1950]
BANKS, ERNIE [1953 – 1971]
CRONIN, JOE [1926 – 1945]
RIPKEN JR., CAL [1981 – PRESENT]
SMITH, OZZIE [1978 – 1996]
WAGNER, HONUS [1897 – 1917]
YOUNT, ROBIN [1974 – 1993]

★

SHORTSTOP

ALL-CENTURY TEAM SHORTSTOP ★ ALL-CENTURY TEAM SHORTSTOP ★ ALL-CENTURY TEAM SHORTSTOP ★ ALL-CENTURY TEAM SHORTSTOP

magine a team with a typical shortstop: good glove, some speed, okay at the plate but not much power. It might be a Mike Bordick, or a Walt Weiss, or a Royce Clayton. Capable and solid, but nothing more. Now imagine that the team acquires a great slugger — a Mo Vaughn or Juan Gonzalez type — who's capable not only of playing shortstop, but of playing it well enough, say, to lead the league in assists, or even to set an all-time record for fielding percentage. This isn't a fantasy; it's the story of the Chicago Cubs' signing of Ernie Banks.

From 1948 to 1953, the Cubs' shortstop was Roy Smalley Sr., whose offensive totals failed to equal even the modest standards of shortstops at that time. Banks joined the team in late 1953 and the following year he became its regular shortstop for the next eight seasons. He was the most dominant hitting shortstop of the live-ball era, giving the Cubs the benefit of one of the league's leading sluggers at a position occupied elsewhere by light hitters. The following table compares Banks' totals during that time to the average of other shortstops pro-rated for the same number of plate appearances as Banks had:

	AB	R	H	2B	3B	HR	RBI	BB	BA	SLG	OBP
BANKS	4,635	748	1,344	209	58	296	852	448	.290	.552	.353
OTHERS	4,606	569	1,187	183	36	66	436	429	.258	.356	.322

During that time, Banks twice led the majors in home runs; no other shortstop in the live-ball era did so even once. His five 40-homer seasons is more than double the total of all other shortstops in major league history combined — at least until Alex Rodriguez next reaches the 40 mark. (He had 38 with two weeks remaining in the 1999 season). Banks led the majors in RBIs twice; the only other shortstop to do so in the live-ball era was Vern Stephens, who also did it twice. And Banks led the majors in extra-base hits four times during that eight-year span. The only players ever to lead the majors more often were Stan Musial (seven times) and Babe Ruth (six).

The names of Vaughn and Gonzalez were chosen because their career batting statistics as of Aug. 31, 1999 were approximations of Banks' from 1954 through 1961 — the closest that exist, in fact, among current players.

	AB	R	H	2B	3B	HR	RBI	BB	SB	BA
BANKS	4,635	748	1,344	209	58	296	852	448	37	.290
VAUGHN	4,241	668	1,274	213	10	252	831	561	28	.300
GONZALEZ	4,719	770	1,377	272	18	331	1055	337	20	.292

CONSECUTIVE MVPs

1958

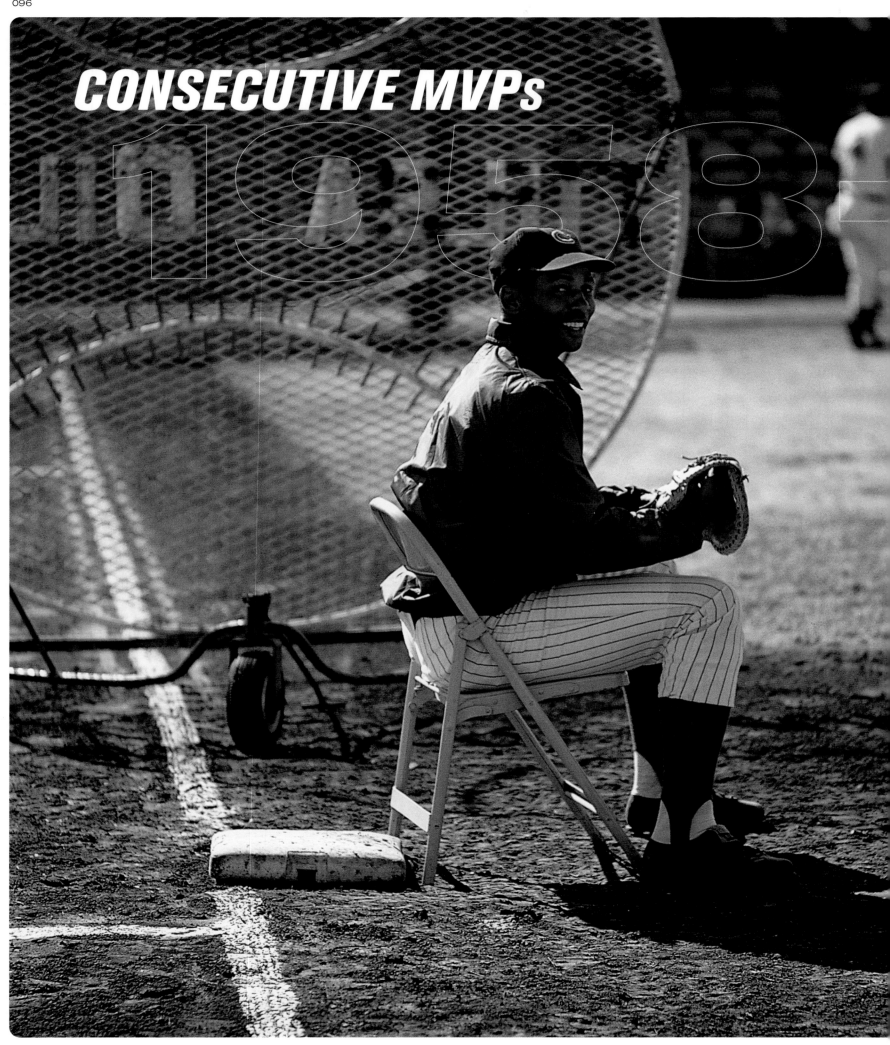

Banks was more than a threat at the plate. As suggested earlier, he led National League shortstops in assists twice (1959 and 1960). And in 1959, he set a major league record for shortstops with a .985 fielding percentage, equivalent to one error every 67 chances, which survived the era of grass fields. It wasn't broken until 1971, when Larry Bowa set a new mark in the Phillies' first season on the artificial turf of Veterans Stadium.

Banks' performance so impressed the voters for the Most Valuable Player award that they bestowed consecutive MVPs on him in 1958 and 1959, despite his team's poor record. (The Cubs were 72-82 in 1958, 74-80 in 1959.) From the inception of the award in its current format in 1931 through 1986, no other player won an MVP award playing for a team with a losing record. Banks did so in consecutive seasons. Two players for losing teams have won MVP awards since then: Andre Dawson and Cal Ripken.

During the first half of his career, Banks was one of the most durable players in the majors. He played shortstop in every Cubs game in four different seasons. A knee injury in the summer of 1961 ended Banks' 717-game playing streak. After a diagnosis that periodic spasms in his left eye impaired his depth perception, Banks was shifted briefly to left field, then to first base for the remainder of his career.

Banks remained an everyday starter for the next eight seasons, but as the next tables show, he couldn't maintain the extraordinary production of his first eight seasons. And even if he had, his impact as a first baseman never could have matched that of a shortstop with comparable offensive value. The comparative figures, with other players pro-rated to reflect the same number of plate appearances as Banks:

BANKS VS. SHORTSTOPS			ERNIE	BANKS VS. 1ST BASEMEN		
BANKS (1954-61)				BANKS (1962-69)		
BA	HR	RBI		BA	HR	RBI
.290	296	852		.260	199	728
OTHER SHORTSTOPS				OTHER 1ST BASEMEN		
BA	HR	RBI		BA	HR	RBI
.258	66	436		.264	163	616

During his eight seasons as a shortstop, Banks ranked third in the majors in home runs, trailing only Mickey Mantle and Eddie Mathews. He ranked second in RBIs to Hank Aaron. Among all players in major league history, only Ralph Kiner and Mathews hit more homers in their first eight seasons than Banks did. With no slight intended to what Banks accomplished during the second half of his career, which included five All-Star Game appearances, his achievements during those eight seasons as a shortstop alone would have been enough to earn a spot on the All-Century Team.

![L]ike the careers of many players on the All-Century Team, Cal Ripken's is defined by one achievement that stands above the rest. In Ripken's case, that signature feat, "The Streak", represents durability and will, but it doesn't reflect the skills or suggest the considerable body of accomplishments that earned him a place on the team.

There's no denying "The Streak " belongs on a short list of baseball's great achievements. For a half-century, Lou Gehrig's streak of 2,130 consecutive games was considered by many to be "unbreakable." It was assumed no one possessed the talent to remain in the lineup, the will to do so and the durability and good fortune to stay there for the 13-plus seasons needed to eclipse Gehrig's mark. That's about as good a description of Cal Ripken and his career as one is likely to find.

PLAYER	BORN	BIRTHPLACE	BATS	THROWS	HEIGHT	WEIGHT	MAJOR LEAGUE DEBUT
CAL RIPKEN, JR.	08/24/60	HAVRE DE GRACE, MD	R	R	6'4"	225	08/10/81

What's amazing in looking back at Ripken's streak isn't only that he persevered for those 13-plus seasons or that he did so at a time when fewer players than ever played even one season without missing a game. It's also the fact he stayed the course long after the previous record had fallen.

There were only 27 players who played an entire season during the 1980s without missing a game. They accounted for a total of 47 "iron-man seasons." Neither total includes the 18 players who didn't miss a game during the strike-shortened 1981 season. Both figures are lows for any decade in the history of major league baseball, despite the fact there were 26 teams during the '80s, compared to 16 for most of the century.

Ripken surprised many observers when he extended his streak another three years after breaking Gehrig's mark. When he finally decided to end it, more than 16 years after it began, he was the only player to have played every game from the point at which he broke Gehrig's mark until then. On that day, his streak of 2,632 games was longer than the next 17 longest current streaks combined! If the additional 502 games

without a miss after breaking Gehrig's mark meant anything, it's that Ripken's streak wasn't just about breaking a record; it was about his ethic.

Besides teaching everyone inside baseball and out a lesson in how to approach one's job, Ripken also was the catalyst for a change that appears to be taking place as the century draws to a close. During the live-ball era, there were few shortstops who hit with power; even fewer who did so and remained shortstops for most of their careers. From 1920 to Ripken's 1982 rookie season, 76 different players hit no home runs in a season in which they played at least 100 games at shortstop. Many did it several times. But only five shortstops hit 25 home runs in a season: Vern Stephens (three times), Ernie Banks (seven times), Woodie Held (once), Rico Petrocelli (twice) and Robin Yount (once). Of those five, only Stephens played the entire prime of his career at shortstop.

Starting with Ripken, baseball began to accept power hitters who were athletic enough to survive at shortstop. And as the 1990s wound down, many teams seemed to embrace such players. Nomar Garciaparra,

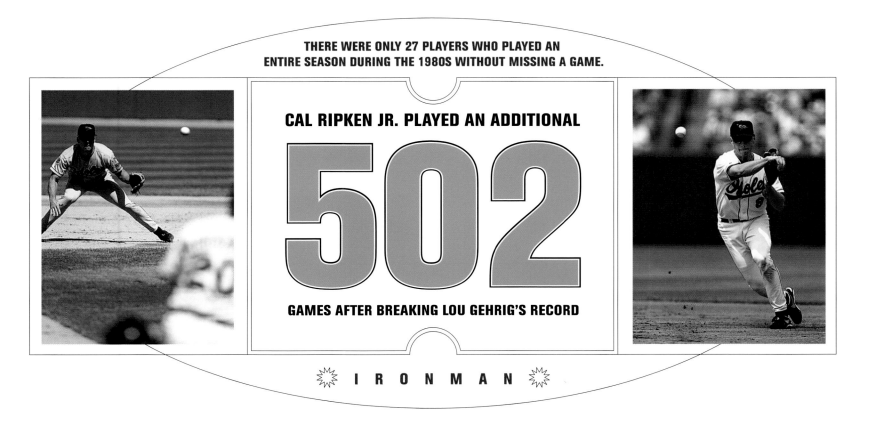

THERE WERE ONLY 27 PLAYERS WHO PLAYED AN ENTIRE SEASON DURING THE 1980S WITHOUT MISSING A GAME.

CAL RIPKEN JR. PLAYED AN ADDITIONAL

502

GAMES AFTER BREAKING LOU GEHRIG'S RECORD

IRONMAN

Alex Rodriguez and Tony Batista all have had at least one 25-HR season and Derek Jeter appears to have the potential to do so. They are all rock-solid at short, considered good to excellent defensively. It took Ripken to blaze the trail, prompted by the confidence of his first major league manager, Earl Weaver.

It was Weaver who took the bold step of shifting Ripken from third base to shortstop. Ripken stood 6-4; 18 of the other 25 teams had shortstops 6-0 or shorter. Beyond that, the Orioles had traded their All-Star third baseman, Doug DeCinces, to clear the path for Ripken. Nevertheless, Weaver said that when he looked at Ripken, he saw a shortstop. Nice call: Ripken went on to set a single-season record for fielding percentage

for shortstops (.996), committing only three errors in 1990. Ripken wasn't only a reliable, error-free fielder; in 1984, he set a record for AL shortstops with 583 assists. He won Gold Glove awards in 1991 and 1992.

It's quite the measure of Ripken's impact on the game that to this point, there has been no mention of his two MVP awards (1983 and 1991) or his streaks of 17 consecutive All-Star Game appearances and 16 consecutive starts that he carries into the new century. Under other circumstances, those would be credentials enough on their own to gain consideration for the All-Century Team — maybe even enough to be selected. In Ripken's case, they are the fine print, because he changed the game in ways that go beyond awards and recognition.

WAGNER, PITTSBURG

HONUS WAGNER

THE MOST VERSATILE PLAYER EVER?

BASED ON WAGNER'S RECORD AND THE VOTE THAT
MADE HIM ONE OF THE CHARTER MEMBERS OF THE HALL
OF FAME, HIS STANDING NEARLY A HALF-CENTURY AGO
SHOULDN'T BE SURPRISING — AT LEAST NOT TO FANS
FAMILIAR WITH HIS RECORD AND THE RESULTS OF THAT
INITIAL HALL OF FAME VOTE. BUT FOR MANY OF TODAY'S
FANS, THOSE ITEMS MIGHT BE OBSCURE. SO A REVIEW OF
HIS ACCOMPLISHMENTS IS IN ORDER.

PLAYER	BORN	BIRTHPLACE	BATS	THROWS	HEIGHT	WEIGHT	MAJOR LEAGUE DEBUT
HONUS WAGNER	02/24/1874	CHARTIERS, PA	R	R	5'11"	200	07/19/1897

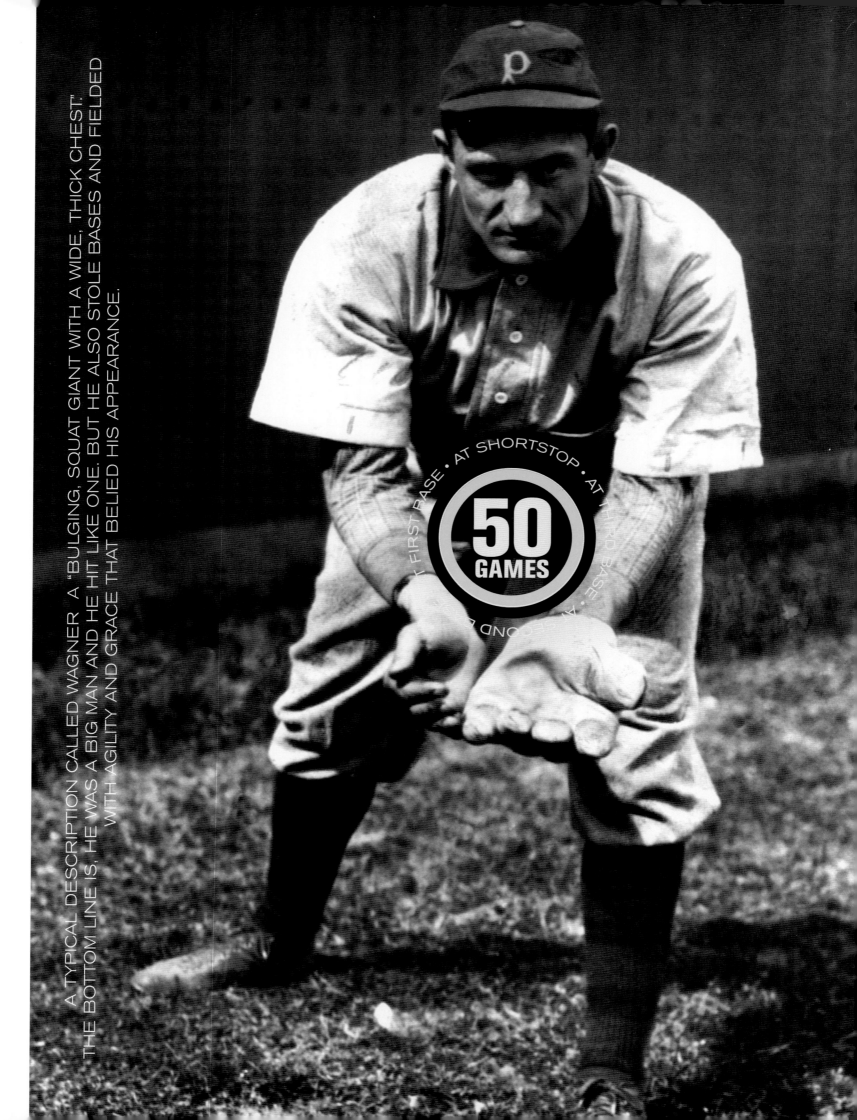

A TYPICAL DESCRIPTION CALLED WAGNER A "BULGING, SQUAT GIANT WITH A WIDE, THICK CHEST." THE BOTTOM LINE IS, HE WAS A BIG MAN AND HE HIT LIKE ONE. BUT HE ALSO STOLE BASES AND FIELDED WITH AGILITY AND GRACE THAT BELIED HIS APPEARANCE.

AT FIRST BASE • AT SHORTSTOP • AT THIRD BASE • AT SECOND B

50 GAMES

irst and foremost, Wagner was an eight-time National League batting champion. He played most of his career at shortstop for the Pittsburgh Pirates, after three seasons at various other positions for the Louisville Colonels (1897-1899). From 1914 to 1923, he was the all-time leader in career hits, a distinction he held among NL players until surpassed by Stan Musial in 1962.

He was moved to shortstop in 1902 and that remained his primary position for 15 years. He was considered a very good shortstop with a great arm. But his versatility was such that he is one of only 29 players in major league history, and the only Hall of Famer, to play at least 50 games at all four infield positions. John McGraw called Wagner the most versatile player he ever had seen.

Wagner was also a great base stealer. His career total of 722 steals ranks ninth in major league history. And his streak of 18 consecutive seasons with 20 or more steals from 1898 to 1915 is the second longest behind Rickey Henderson's ongoing streak of 21 years.

And so when a committee voted in 1936 on the players to be included in the Hall of Fame's first induction, Wagner was one of five to be selected. Among those five, he got more votes than the two pitchers — Walter Johnson and Christy Mathewson — and the same number as Babe Ruth. Only Ty Cobb received more votes than Wagner among an electorate who had seen them all play. So why have Wagner's accomplishments become obscure? Why has his standing fallen?

Wagner played much of his career in the deadest part of the dead-ball era — a time when offense had ebbed even by turn-of-the-century standards. The NL batting average during Wagner's career, with each season weighted for his number of at-bats, was .259; the slugging percentage was .339. Those are the approximate career averages of light-hitting contemporary infielders such as Ricky Guitierrez and Harold Reynolds. In this universe of Mike Bordicks, Wagner's career averages were .329 and .469, respectively. Put another way, in Wagner's day batting average was a truer offensive measure than it is today, because the extra-base power it ignores was less a factor. This makes his eight batting titles all the more significant.

Taken at face value, measures of Wagner's fielding are also irrelevant to the point of being misleading when compared to those of

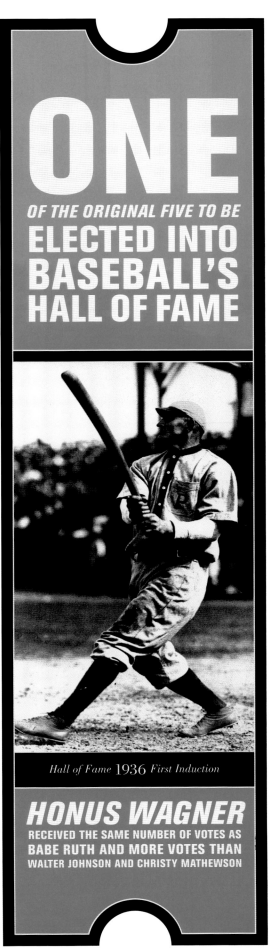

Hall of Fame 1936 *First Induction*

HONUS WAGNER
RECEIVED THE SAME NUMBER OF VOTES AS BABE RUTH AND MORE VOTES THAN WALTER JOHNSON AND CHRISTY MATHEWSON

ONE OF THE ORIGINAL FIVE TO BE **ELECTED INTO BASEBALL'S HALL OF FAME**

other 20th-century Hall of Fame shortstops. He made an average of 44 errors per season during 14 years from 1903 to 1916 — more per season than Cal Ripken made in his five best seasons combined! But that was simply a reflection of Wagner's times. In fact, he had a higher fielding percentage (that is, a lower rate of errors) than the league average in each of those 14 years.

Maybe the best indication of Wagner's defensive ability is the fact that he was still playing shortstop regularly in his 40s. He played a total of 356 games at shortstop in his 40s — not only a record, but nearly four times as many as runner-up Ozzie Smith. Shortstops were considered even more important defensively then than they are today. Assuming that his defense declined with age — and if it didn't, he's even more special than we think — for Wagner to have played capably in his 40s suggests he must have been magnificent in his 20s and 30s.

Wagner's durability is underlined by the fact that in 1915, at the age of 41, he played all 156 games for the Pirates — the oldest "iron-man" season in MLB history.

Finally, Wagner may have been one of those players you had to see to appreciate fully. Recaps of his career often refer to his unusual appearance, sometimes in bluntly insensitive ways.

Clearly, Wagner had an unusual and stocky build. He was 5-11 and 200 pounds, much larger than the typical player of his day. The league average was 5-10, 172 pounds; the other shortstops were considerably smaller than that: 5-9, 163 pounds.

We can only imagine how Wagner must have appeared to fans of 100 years ago. A typical description called him a "bulging, squat giant with a wide, thick chest." The bottom line is, Wagner was a big man, and he hit like one. But he also stole bases and fielded with agility and grace that belied his appearance.

Still, for all that, the top line on Wagner's resume has to be his eight batting titles, a National League record equaled only by Tony Gwynn. There weren't MVP awards or Gold Gloves or All-Star appearances in Wagner's day to help keep alive the memory of how great a player he was. But we do have that first Hall of Fame vote, by his contemporaries, that placed him in the most elite company baseball has to offer. There seems little question that Wagner was one of the game's greatest players. It could be that he is now also one of its most underrated.

★

FOXX, JIMMIE [1925–1945]
GEHRIG, LOU [1923–1939]
GREENBERG, HANK [1930–1947]
KILLEBREW, HARMON [1954–1975]
LEONARD, BUCK [1934–1948]
MCCOVEY, WILLIE [1959–1980]
MCGWIRE, MARK [1986–PRESENT]
MURRAY, EDDIE [1977–1997]
SISLER, GEORGE [1915–1930]
TERRY, BILL [1923–1936]

★

FIRST BASE

ALL-CENTURY TEAM ★ FIRST BASE

2130

LOU GEHRIG

FOR SEVERAL GENERATIONS OF BASEBALL FANS, LOU GEHRIG'S ACCOMPLISHMENTS WERE OBSCURED BY THE GLOW OF ONE THE MOST FAMILIAR AND RESPECTED NUMBERS IN SPORTS: TWENTY-ONE THIRTY. LONG CITED AS ONE OF THE TWO MOST UNBREAKABLE RECORDS IN BASEBALL, GEHRIG'S STREAK OF 2130 CONSECUTIVE GAMES PLAYED DEFINED HIS CAREER AS FEW NUMBERS HAVE MARKED THE CAREERS OF ANY OTHER ATHLETES.

There was a certain irony when Gehrig's playing streak was surpassed by Cal Ripken in 1995. That's because despite all his accomplishments, Gehrig was one of baseball's most prolific runners-up. He finished second in the American League in home runs four times and he ranked second in RBIs four times as well. Only Mel Ott was a league runner-up in home runs more often (7); Gehrig shares the mark for ranking second in RBIs with Ott, Frank Robinson and Babe Ruth.

PLAYER	BORN	BIRTHPLACE	BATS	THROWS	HEIGHT	WEIGHT	MAJOR LEAGUE DEBUT
LOU GEHRIG	06/19/03	NEW YORK, NY	L	L	6'	200	06/15/23

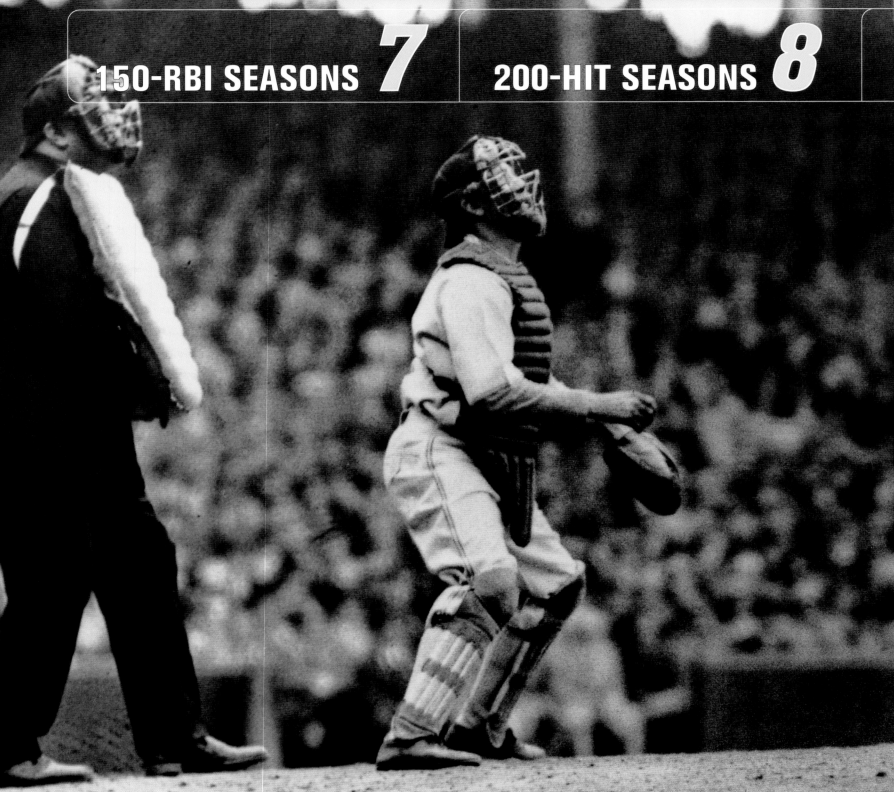

150-RBI SEASONS 7

200-HIT SEASONS 8

But viewed apart from the feats of his teammate Ruth and his soulmate Ripken, Gehrig's consistency and excellence earned him a place in the highest levels of baseball achievement. For 13 straight seasons from 1926 through 1938, Gehrig scored and drove in at least 100 runs. Not only is that the longest such streak in major league history, but in most seasons Gehrig shattered both those totals. He actually drove in and scored

at least 125 runs in 10 of those seasons, including eight straight (1927-1934). No other player ever has had a streak even half that long! Gehrig had more 150-RBI seasons than anyone else (7). He had three seasons in which his slugging percentage was in the .700s, though typically he ranked second to Ruth in two of them. And get this: Gehrig had eight 200-hit seasons, a total matched only by singles hitters or stars of the

RUTH AND GEHRIG ARE THE ONLY TEAMMATES EVER TO PLAY AT LEAST 10 SEASONS TOGETHER AND TO COMBINE FOR 700 HOME RUNS DURING THAT 10-YEAR PERIOD. THEY BELTED A TOTAL OF 771 HOMERS FROM 1925 THROUGH 1934, FAR SURPASSING THE NEXT-HIGHEST TOTALS – 692 BY EDDIE MATHEWS AND HANK AARON (1954 TO 1963) AND 675 BY WILLIE MAYS AND WILLIE MCCOVEY (1960 TO 1969).

.700+ SLUGGING PERCENTAGE SEASONS 3

dead-ball era: Pete Rose, 10; Ty Cobb, 9; Willie Keeler and Paul Waner, 8. Gehrig hit more home runs (493) than those four players combined (424).

Gehrig also drove in 35 runs in his first 30 World Series games. No other player in postseason history averaged more than an RBI per game over a span of 30 games. Even Mr. October, Reggie Jackson, maxed out at 30 RBIs in 30 games (1977-1982); Ruth's best 30-game total was 26.

So now, more than a half-century after his retirement and his untimely death, Gehrig becomes a runner-up to Ripken in the one way in which he once seemed untouchable. With the focus now off his playing streak, what an odd twist it would be if Gehrig now were appreciated for his enormous accomplishments in those 2,130 games (plus 34 others) rather than for simply having played in them.

JUST WHEN YOU THINK SOCIETY HAS BECOME TOO JADED OR CYNICAL, NO LONGER CAPABLE OF THE KIND OF ADULATION ONCE ACCORDED TO RUTH, ALONG COMES AN ALI, A JORDAN. CAN MCGWIRE REACH THAT LEVEL?

MARK McGWIRE

WHO WAS THE GREATEST HOME RUN HITTER OF THE 20TH CENTURY?

FOR MOST OF THE PAST 70 YEARS, THAT QUESTION WAS
SETTLED BEYOND DISPUTE. IT WAS BABE RUTH.
AS THE CENTURY ENDS, IT'S STILL BEYOND DISPUTE.
THE ANSWER IS NOW MARK MCGWIRE.

The proof is in the numbers. McGwire didn't just edge past Maris' record, nor was he the latest in a series of serious challengers to Maris' long-standing mark — the one among equals who just happened to reach 62. He broke Maris' record with 18 games to spare, then added eight more home runs during that time. McGwire did that despite the fact for the first 35 years of Maris' reign, there were absolutely no serious challengers to the record. Until McGwire and Junior Griffey did so in 1997, no one had come within eight home runs of Maris' mark.

PLAYER	BORN	BIRTHPLACE	BATS	THROWS	HEIGHT	WEIGHT	MAJOR LEAGUE DEBUT
MARK McGWIRE	10/01/63	POMONA, CA	R	R	6'5"	225	08/22/86

But even that is a too-narrow focus on the enormity of what McGwire achieved. It's true, he did break the most hallowed single-season mark in *The Book Of Baseball Records*. But the record-breaking season was "merely" the high point of a five-year home run assault that began in 1995 and which transcended everything that came before it, including the best of Ruth, Maris, Hank Aaron, or any other previous home-run champ.

Ruth hit one home run for every 11.8 at-bats over his career. Until McGwire's arrival, that average not only stood as the all-time record, but it appeared to be one of those untouchable "super records" in that it was 20 percent higher than that of the runner-up, Ralph Kiner (one per 14.1 ABs).

Not only has McGwire surpassed Ruth's average, he did so with a years-long fireworks display during which he hit one home run every 8.2 at-bats (his average from 1995 through 1998). That is 22 percent higher than the best four-year span of Ruth's career (1926-1929); and 44 percent higher than Ruth's career mark — you know, the one that looked unapproachable for the half-century before McGwire's arrival. For emphasis:

44 percent higher than a previously unapproachable standard.

That doesn't even include McGwire's performance in 1999. As we went to press, Big Mac was launching a run at his own year-old record. With two weeks to play in the '99 season, McGwire already had hit 58 home runs raising his total to 277 for the five-year period starting in 1995, exceeding Ruth's record for homers over five seasons (256 from 1926 to 1930).

It remains unlikely that anyone ever could shatter home-run records to the same arithmetic degree as Ruth did in the 1920s — unless, that is, the ball (or bat, or stadiums) is changed in some similarly radical way. But the degree to which McGwire has shattered home run marks that stood for decades — some of which seemed untouchable on that count alone — suggests he has crossed a line between what is remarkable and what would have been considered impossible had we not seen him do it. That's the same line Ruth crossed 70 years earlier and helped make him a legend.

Even Ruth's unlikely path to home run glory is echoed somewhat by

HOME RUNS PER AT-BATS **RUTH** 1920 ONE PER **8.5** 1921 ONE PER **9.2** 1927 ONE PER **9.0**

McGwire's. As documented in this book, Ruth not only launched his major league career as a pitcher, but he was a great one at an early age. It's not the fact McGwire was also a pitcher (which he was at USC) that reminds us most of Ruth, but simply that five years into his career, it appeared unlikely McGwire's potential to break home run records would be realized.

As a rookie, McGwire already was setting home run marks. His total of 49 homers in 1987 shattered a 57-year-old mark of 38 home runs set by Wally Berger in 1930 and equaled by Frank Robinson in 1956. No rookie has ever come within 10 homers of McGwire's mark. His total of 156 home runs after four seasons (through 1990) ranked second in history to Ralph Kiner's 168. But in 1991, Mac hit only 22 home runs and his batting average fell to .201.

Subsequent seasons compromised by chronic injuries and a players' strike also took their toll. McGwire had only 219 at-bats combined in 1993 and 1994. But when baseball resumed in 1995, Mark McGwire and his unrealized potential had given way to Big Mac. To that point, the three highest single-season home run rates all belonged to Babe Ruth: one per 8.5 at-bats in 1920; one per 9.0 ABs in 1927; and one per 9.2 ABs in 1921. McGwire broke the record in 1995 (8.1). In fact, it's McGwire who now holds the three highest marks in major-league history, having surpassed Ruth's best average again in 1996 and setting a new record in 1998 (one per 7.3 ABs). Given what McGuire did in the first five months of 1999, he had a chance to hold the top four spots.

Trying to predict how future generations will view our own is tricky at best. For Mark McGwire to become to the 21st century what Babe Ruth was to the 20th may be setting too high a standard. But just when you think society has become too jaded or cynical, no longer capable of the kind of adulation once accorded to Ruth, along comes an Ali, a Jordan. Can McGwire reach that level? It's too early to say. But like Ruth, Ali and Jordan, he hasn't merely broken records; he has shattered the existing view of what is possible. And in so doing he invites the comparison to those legends.

IN ONE SEASON

MCGWIRE ⟩ 1995 ⟩ ONE PER 8.1 ⟩ 1996 ⟩ ONE PER 7.3 ⟩ 1998 ⟩ ONE PER 8.2

★

CAREW, ROD [1967–1985]
COLLINS, EDDIE [1906–1930]
FRISCH, FRANKIE [1919–1937]
GEHRINGER, CHARLIE [1924–1942]
HORNSBY, ROGERS [1915–1937]
LAJOIE, NAPOLEON [1896–1916]
MORGAN, JOE [1963–1984]
ROBINSON, JACKIE [1947–1956]

★

SECOND
BASE

ALL-CENTURY TEAM SECOND BASE ★ ALL-CENTURY TEAM SECOND BASE ★ ALL-CENTURY TEAM SECOND BASE ★ ALL-CENTURY TEAM SECOND BASE ★ ALL-CENTURY TEAM SECOND BASE

THE TWO MOST DOMINANT HITTERS OF THE FIRST DECADE OF THE LIVE-BALL ERA WERE BABE RUTH AND ROGERS HORNSBY. AS MUCH AS RUTH STOOD HEAD-AND-SHOULDERS ABOVE ALL OTHERS DURING THE 1920S, HORNSBY WAS JUST AS CLEARLY THE SECOND BEST.

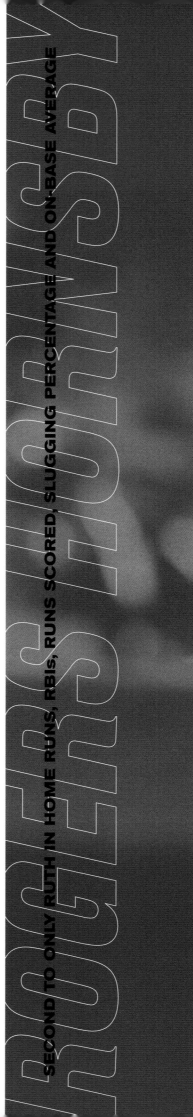

ROGERS HORNSBY

SECOND TO ONLY RUTH IN HOME RUNS, RBIs, RUNS SCORED, SLUGGING PERCENTAGE AND ON-BASE AVERAGE

R uth led the majors in home runs, RBIs, runs scored, slugging percentage and on-base average. Hornsby ranked second in all of them and he led the majors by a wide margin in batting average with a .382 mark. Only two players were within even 25 points: Harry Heilmann (.364) and Ty Cobb (.357).

Even more impressive is Hornsby's total of 2,085 hits during the 1920s, the highest 10-year total in this century, topped only once before that. Willie Keller had 2,095 hits from 1894 through 1903. Six players with more than 3,000 career hits never reached 208 hits even once: Honus Wagner, Carl Yastrzemski, Eddie Murray, Dave Winfield, Lou Brock and Al Kaline. Hornsby averaged 208 hits over a 10-year period, during which he also led the National League in home runs by a margin so wide that only one player was within 100 of his total. Hornsby hit 250 homers during the '20s; NL runner-up Cy Williams hit 202.

PLAYER	BORN	BIRTHPLACE	BATS	THROWS	HEIGHT	WEIGHT	MAJOR LEAGUE DEBUT
ROGERS HORNSBY	04/27/1896	WINTERS, TX	R	R	5'11"	175	09/10/15

.424

BATTING AVERAGE IN 1924

HORNSBY'S .424 BATTING AVERAGE IN 1924 NOT ONLY REMAINS THE HIGHEST OF THE LIVE-BALL ERA, IT WILL LIVE FOREVER AS THE BEST OF THE 20TH CENTURY, EVEN INCLUDING THE FIRST TWO DECADES WHEN THERE WERE MORE .400 HITTERS (4) THAN THERE WERE 20-HR SEASONS (3).

Hornsby had three of the top 11 averages of the century and eight of his 10 batting averages during the 1920s rank among the top 100. In 1922, he became the first player ever with 100 singles and 100 extra-base hits in the same season, a feat accomplished by only four others after him (Lou Gehrig and Chuck Klein twice each, Jimmie Foxx and Stan Musial).

Hornsby is the only second baseman during the live-ball era to lead the majors in extra-base hits (three times), home runs (twice) or RBIs (1925).

He became the all-time National League home run leader in 1929 and stayed atop the list until 1937, when he was passed by Mel Ott on his way to 511. Hornsby's .358 batting average ranks second in major league history only to Ty Cobb (.367). Although Ryne Sandberg broke his record for home runs as a second baseman, Hornsby's total of 301 is the highest among players who spent most of their careers as second basemen. (The difference is because of Hornsby's first five seasons when he played mostly shortstop and third base.)

Hornsby's record might have been even greater were it not for a foot injury that limited him to 104 at-bats in 1930. Coming off a 1929 season in which he batted .380 and hit 39 homers at the age of 33, he may have assumed he had another five or six prime years ahead. But Hornsby's last season as even a semi-regular starter was 1931, when he played a modest 100 games and posted good, if not Rajah-like, numbers (.331, 16 HR in 357 AB).

FIRST 100/100 PLAYER

An interesting sidelight to Hornsby's career is the frequency with which he was passed around from team to team. Given his standing as the league's best hitter, it's shocking to see he spent each of the four years from 1926 to 1929 with a different team — the Cardinals, Giants, Braves and Cubs, respectively. Few players in this century have started regularly for a different team in each of four consecutive seasons. Among those who did, several were free agents who changed teams at least once by their own choice, an option not available until 1976 (e.g., Oscar Gamble, Luis Gonzalez, Otis Nixon). The fact that the often troublesome Dick Allen was traded around like Hornsby (Phillies to Cardinals to Dodgers to White Sox from 1969 to 1972) may help put Rajah's own tem-

perament into perspective. The literature of his time made it clear Hornsby was an unpleasant and boorish man — so much so, it appears, that two teams dumped him at the first opportunity despite coming off seasons in which he batted in the .360s! That's a lot of unpleasantness.

Ultimately, Hornsby's place in history is that of the National League's answer to Babe Ruth. No one could match the Bambino either at the plate or for sheer force of personality. But at a time when league identities were much stronger than today, Hornsby provided the NL with a great hitter by almost any standard other than the Ruth standard.

JACKIE ROBINSON

GIVEN HIS ROLE AS THE TRAILBLAZER FOR THE MOST SIGNIFICANT CHANGE IN THE HISTORY OF MAJOR LEAGUE BASEBALL — THE MOST IMPORTANT IN THE HISTORY OF AMERICAN SOCIETY, SOME HAVE SAID — IT'S EASY TO OVERLOOK HOW GREAT A BASEBALL PLAYER JACKIE ROBINSON WAS.

That's especially true for those who didn't see him play, whose vision of Robinson the player is by the glare of Robinson, the man who broke baseball's color line. The problem is compounded by the difficulty of judging Robinson's abilities according to the statistical record he left behind. As good as that record is — Rookie of the Year in 1947, Most Valuable Player in 1949, six-time All-Star, etc. — it doesn't do justice to his ability and impact as a player, especially when his statistics are judged by today's standards.

So, with no disrespect to his importance as a pioneer, let's take a look at Robinson as he might have been viewed in a more perfect world: as a ballplayer, simply that, and one of the greatest of the century.

During Robinson's 10-year major league career, all spent with the Dodgers, Brooklyn scored an average of 5.3 runs per game. That's the highest 10-year average by any National League team in the last 60 years. Over the last four years of that period, Duke Snider, Gil Hodges, Roy Campanella and Carl Furillo hit 498 home runs — the highest four-year total by four teammates in NL history outside of Coors Field.

But on this scoring machine, with an unparalleled quartet of home-run sluggers, the Dodgers' cleanup hitter for much of that time was their second baseman, Jackie Robinson. Of Robinson's nearly 5,000 career at-bats, 51 percent were from the cleanup slot; he batted cleanup in 21 of Brooklyn's 39 World Series games in that span. His position in such a powerful batting order is a telling measure of respect for his run production — one that's surprising, given his greater reputation for wreaking havoc on the basepaths.

Robinson wasn't merely a symbolic Rookie of the Year in 1947, the first year in which the award was based on a national vote of baseball writers. He scored 125 runs, a total matched by only two rookies since then (Junior Gilliam in 1953 and Dick Allen in 1964 — both of them rookie-award winners), surpassed by none. He fell two hits short of the .300 mark; ranked second among rookies to Bobby Thomson with 48 extra-base hits; and led the NL in stolen bases (29). His only real competition in the voting was Giants pitcher Larry Jansen, who posted a 21-5 record.

PLAYER	BORN	BIRTHPLACE	BATS	THROWS	HEIGHT	WEIGHT	MAJOR LEAGUE DEBUT
JACKIE ROBINSON	01/31/19	STAMFORD, CT	R	R	5'11"	204	04/15/47

That was for starters. From 1947 through 1953, Robinson's first seven years, he ranked fourth in the majors in batting average (.319), second in runs scored (773), and first in steals (166). In his MVP season of 1949, Robinson combined batting skill, productivity and speed in a way that few others have. Only one player in the live-ball era matched his figures in batting average (.342), RBIs (124), and stolen bases (37) in the same season: Kiki Cuyler in 1930.

Still, despite all this, Robinson never hit 20 home runs, never stole 40 bases and failed to reach any of the prominent career totals such as 3,000 hits that many other members of the All-Century team attained. Then again, Robinson didn't make his major league debut until the age of 28, sacrificing five seasons or more to the prejudices of that era.

By using a similar-players technique, we have tried to reconstruct what Robinson's page in the *Baseball Encyclopedia* might have looked like had the color barrier fallen before his time. Although our projections are based on several dozen players, contributing in proportion to their similarity to Robinson's 1947 statistics, one stood out for its likeness:

YR	PLAYER	G	AB	R	H	2B	3B	HR	RBI	BB	SO	SB	BA
1947	JACKIE ROBINSON	151	590	125	175	31	5	12	48	74	36	29	.297
1979	BILL MADLOCK	154	560	85	167	26	5	14	85	52	41	32	.298

We highlight the Robinson-Madlock similarity here to make an important point: Players simply don't have seasons such as Robinson's at age 28 unless they were ready to play in the majors long before, and to do it at an All-Star level. Madlock, who was 28 in 1979, is a telling example, if an extreme one. By 1979, he had already posted five .300 seasons and won a pair of batting titles. Some of the other more prominent 28-year-olds who compiled similar seasons are listed in the following table:

YR	PLAYER	G	AB	R	H	2B	3B	HR	RBI	BB	SO	SB	BA
1947	JACKIE ROBINSON	151	590	125	175	31	5	12	48	74	36	29	.297
1952	BOBBY AVILA	150	597	102	179	26	11	7	45	67	36	12	.300
1978	KEN GRIFFEY	158	614	90	177	33	8	10	63	54	70	23	.288
1984	ROBIN YOUNT	160	624	105	186	27	7	16	80	67	67	14	.298
1985	PAUL MOLITOR	140	576	93	171	28	3	10	48	54	80	21	.297

By building a composite of the early careers of players most similar at age 28 to Robinson, and adjusting for differences between Robinson and the group in general, we built the following projection for Robinson's career before 1947. When combined with his actual totals from 1947 on, the record of his performance more accurately represents his abilities on the field — an across-the-board combination of speed, power and pure hitting ability:

YRS	G	AB	R	H	2B	3B	HR	RBI	BB	SO	SB	BA
1941-1946	595	2231	419	634	101	18	34	157	299	91	113	.284
1947-1956	1382	4877	947	1518	273	54	137	734	740	291	197	.311
TOTALS	1977	7108	1366	2152	374	72	171	891	1039	382	310	.303

Rightfully so, the focus on Jackie Robinson always will be on the courage and fortitude he showed in opening the major leagues to African-Americans. But just as historians have labored to understand and describe a man as complex as Robinson, baseball historians always will find it difficult to identify and express his abilities on the field with traditional tools. More than any other player in the history of baseball, a sport rightfully proud of its rich statistical heritage, Robinson the player cannot be measured only in numbers — no matter how great.

JACKIE ROBINSON: THE PLAYER CANNOT BE MEASURED ONLY IN NUMBERS—NO MATTER HOW GREAT.

★

AARON, HANK [1954–1976]
BELL, COOL PAPA [1922–1946]
BONDS, BARRY [1986–PRESENT]
BROCK, LOU [1961–1979]
CHARLESTON, OSCAR [1915–1941]
CLEMENTE, ROBERTO [1955–1972]
COBB, TY [1905–1928]
DIMAGGIO, JOE [1936–1951]
GOSLIN, GOOSE [1921–1938]
GRIFFEY JR., KEN [1989–PRESENT]
GWYNN, TONY [1982–PRESENT]
HEILMANN, HARRY [1914–1932]
HENDERSON, RICKEY [1979–PRESENT]
JACKSON, JOE [1908–1920]
JACKSON, REGGIE [1967–1987]
KALINE, AL [1953–1974]
KEELER, WILLIE [1892–1910]
KINER, RALPH [1946–1955]
MANTLE, MICKEY [1951–1968]
MAYS, WILLIE [1951–1973]
MEDWICK, JOE [1932–1948]
MUSIAL, STAN [1941–1963]
OTT, MEL [1926–1947]
ROBINSON, FRANK [1956–1976]
ROSE, PETE [1963–1986]
RUTH, BABE [1914–1935]
SIMMONS, AL [1924–1944]
SNIDER, DUKE [1947–1964]
SPEAKER, TRIS [1907–1928]
STARGELL, WILLIE [1962–1982]
WANER, PAUL [1926–1945]
WILLIAMS, BILLY [1959–1976]
WILLIAMS, TED [1939–1960]
YASTRZEMSKI, CARL [1961–1983]

★

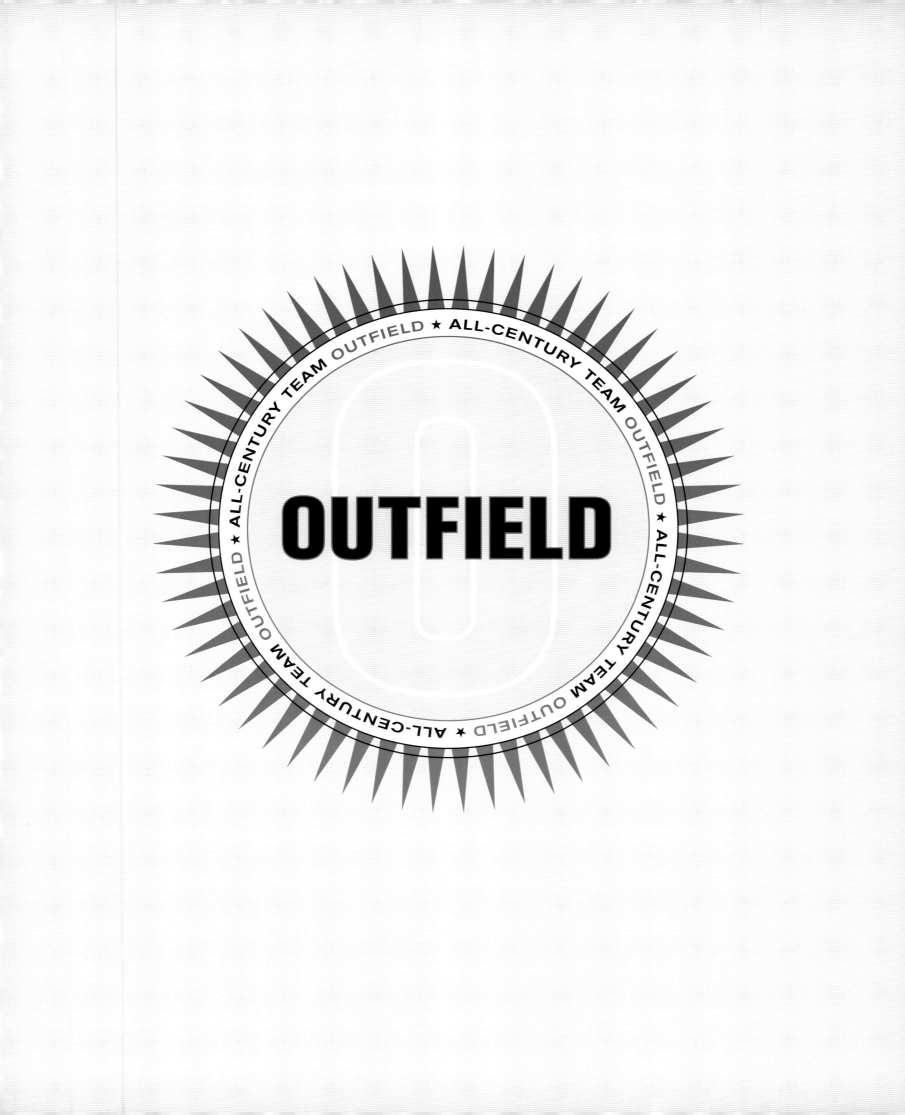

OUTFIELD

IMAGINE A PLAYER GOOD ENOUGH TO BE ELECTED TO BASEBALL'S
HALL OF FAME DESPITE HAVING ONLY AVERAGE POWER. HE WOULD HAVE TO BE
A GREAT HITTER WITH A LONG, PRODUCTIVE CAREER — SOMEONE WITH
EXCEPTIONAL ON-BASE AND EXTRA-BASE POTENTIAL AND A GOOD BASE STEALER.
CERTAINLY IT WOULD HELP IF HE WERE THE BEST FIELDER AT HIS POSITION.

NOW TAKE THAT PLAYER AND MAKE HIM THE GREATEST
HOME-RUN HITTER IN MAJOR LEAGUE HISTORY AND THE ONE PLAYER WHO
DROVE IN MORE RUNS THAN ANY OTHER. THAT PLAYER IS HANK AARON.

	BA	2B	3B	HR	RBI	BB	SB
HANK AARON	.305	624	98		2297	1402	240
GEORGE BRETT	.305	665	137	317	1595	1096	201
TY COBB	.367	724	297	117	1961	1249	892
CHARLIE GEHRINGER	.320	574	146	184	1427	1185	182
WILLIE MAYS	.302	523	140	660	1903	1463	338
PAUL MOLITOR	.306	605	114	234	1307	1094	504
PETE ROSE	.303	746	135	160	1314	1566	198
TRIS SPEAKER	.344	793	223	117	1559	1381	433

he fact is that there are only seven .300-hitters who had even three-quarters of Aaron's career totals in doubles, triples, walks and stolen bases.

Of those seven, only Mays hit even half as many home runs as Aaron did. Only Mays and Cobb came within 700 RBIs of Aaron's total (including reconstructed RBI totals for Cobb before 1920 when the category was first compiled officially). Yet based on totals comparable to those of Aaron, but in general lacking his power and production, five of the seven are in the Hall of Fame, and the other two are currently ineligible (Molitor and Rose).

PLAYER	BORN	BIRTHPLACE	BATS	THROWS	HEIGHT	WEIGHT	MAJOR LEAGUE DEBUT
HANK AARON	02/05/34	MOBILE, AB	R	R	6'	180	04/13/54

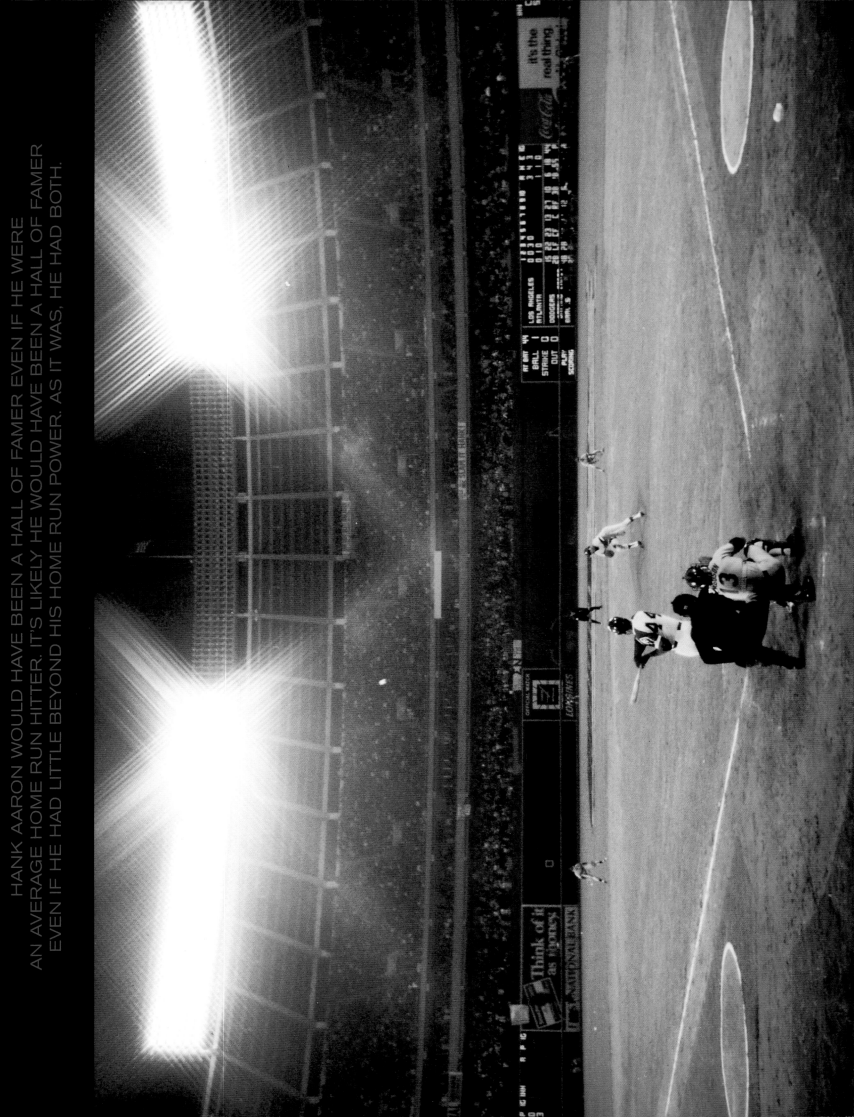

HANK AARON WOULD HAVE BEEN A HALL OF FAMER EVEN IF HE WERE AN AVERAGE HOME RUN HITTER. IT'S LIKELY HE WOULD HAVE BEEN A HALL OF FAMER EVEN IF HE HAD LITTLE BEYOND HIS HOME RUN POWER. AS IT WAS, HE HAD BOTH.

755 HOME RUNS

PLAYER	AT AGE 30	AT AGE 35	AT AGE 40	TOTAL
RUTH	284	516	708	714
AARON	342	510	713	755
MAYS	285	512	633	660
MCGWIRE*	229	457	512+	
GRIFFEY*	395+			

* MARK MCGWIRE WAS 36 AND KEN GRIFFEY JR 29 AT THE END OF THE 1999 SEASON.

+ TOTALS WITH TWO WEEKS REMAINING IN THE 1999 SEASON.

200 HOME RUNS FROM AGE 35 TO 40

Keep in mind that Aaron was also a three-time winner of the Gold Glove Award, winning as many as Rose, Brett and Molitor combined. (Mays won 12 Gold Gloves; Cobb, Charlie Gehringer and Tris Speaker played before the award was instituted.)

The conclusion: Hank Aaron would have been a Hall of Famer even if he were an average home run hitter. It's likely he would have been a Hall of Famer even if he had little beyond his home run power. As it was, he had both.

For the first time since Aaron's assault on Babe Ruth's career home run record, the possibility of challengers to his own record looms. Ken Griffey Jr. has established an all-time record for home runs by the age of 30; and Mark McGwire has demonstrated the ability to narrow the gap separating him from Aaron faster than any player before him.

But like a marathon runner setting a blazing pace and aiming to break a record that once seemed untouchable, Griffey and McGwire, and maybe others in time to come, are about to confront a daunting reality. Not only did Aaron himself set a fast pace, but when others were struggling simply to maintain their pace, he went into overdrive. During the five years from age 35 to 40, Aaron hit more than 200 home runs —

an average of more than 40 per season.

Only Ruth himself has come within 50 home runs of Aaron's total during that time. The top 10 from age 35 to 40: Aaron, 203; Ruth, 192; Ted Williams, 148; Darrell Evans, 133; Cy Williams, 126; Mike Schmidt, 124; Reggie Jackson, 122; Andre Dawson, Carlton Fisk, and Willie Mays, 121.

In the late 1960s, Mays and Aaron were considered about equally likely to challenge or break Ruth's record. But Aaron became the one based on his late charge. The table above shows career home run totals at various ages for some past and future challengers. Note that at the age of 35, Ruth, Aaron and Mays were separated over the course of their careers by less than a month's worth of homers.

For years, would-be challengers to Ruth's record of 60 home runs in a season fell by the wayside as they failed to match the Babe's total of 17 homers during September — still a record for the month, equaled only once (by Albert Belle in 1995). Similarly, as contenders appear to have Aaron's record in their sights, the toughest part of the battle might still lie ahead for them, based on Aaron's unprecedented power display in his late 30s.

BEFORE THE ARRIVAL OF THE LIVE BALL AND THE ADVENT OF BASEBALL'S HOME RUN ERA, BATTING WAS A SCIENCE. HOME RUNS WERE AN OCCASIONAL EXCITING DIVERSION BUT THEY DID NOT DISTRACT ATTENTION FROM WHAT MADE A PLAYER A "GOOD HITTER." IT WAS IN THAT CONTEXT THAT BATTING AVERAGE BECAME THE MEASURE OF A HITTER, EXPLAINING WHY TY COBB TO THIS DAY IS CONSIDERED BY MANY TO BE THE GREATEST "BATSMAN" EVER TO PLAY THE GAME.

T he litany is impressive. Cobb led the American League in batting average 12 times over a 13-year period from 1907 to 1919. His record streak of 23 consecutive seasons batting .300 or better spanned nearly his entire career, including all but his first season when he batted .240 in just 150 at-bats. And even though his "power" looks suspect because he played most of his career in the dead-ball era, he was among his day's top home run hitters.

Another way to look at the same feat: No player has ever led his league in hits, home runs, runs scored, RBIs, walks, or stolen bases 12 times in 13 seasons. No pitcher has ever "gone 12-for-13" in wins,

shutouts, complete games, earned run average, strikeouts, or saves. Some came close, though in categories of lesser importance than batting average. Rickey Henderson led the AL in steals 11 times in 12 years. Walter Johnson went 11-for-13 in strikeouts. But no one dominated a major category as Cobb did in the one category that's synonymous with batting.

To say that Cobb's streak of 23 straight .300 seasons, from 1906 through 1928, is the longest in major league history doesn't do him justice. First, it was not just the longest, it was six seasons longer than the second-longest streaks — 17 in a row by Honus Wagner (1897-1913), Ted Williams (1939-1958), and Stan Musial (1941-1958).

PLAYER	BORN	BIRTHPLACE	BATS	THROWS	HEIGHT	WEIGHT	MAJOR LEAGUE DEBUT
TY COBB	12/18/1886	NARROWS, GA	L	R	6'1"	175	08/30/05

LET'S LOOK AT THOSE ACHIEVEMENTS INDIVIDUALLY. IN 1990, GEORGE BRETT EARNED RECOGNITION FOR LEADING THE AMERICAN LEAGUE IN HITTING, BECOMING THE ONLY PLAYER TO LEAD HIS LEAGUE IN THREE DIFFERENT DECADES (I.E., THE '70S, '80S AND '90S). TO WIN BATTING TITLES 14 YEARS APART, AS BRETT DID, REPRESENTS NEARLY UNPRECEDENTED LONGEVITY OF EXCELLENCE. BUT WHAT DOES THAT SAY OF COBB'S ACCOMPLISHMENT? NOT ONLY DID HE WIN TITLES SPANNING 13 YEARS, BUT HE WON 12 TITLES DURING THAT PERIOD, COMPARED TO BRETT'S THREE (1976, 1980 AND 1990).

23 STRAIGHT .300+ SEASONS

BATTING TITLES

BRETT

1976	1977	1978	1979	1980	1981	1982	1983	1984	1985	1986	1987	1988	1989	1990
.333	.312	.294	.329	.390	.314	.301	.310	.284	.335	.290	.290	.306	.282	.329

COBB

1907	1908	1909	1910	1911	1912	1913	1914	1915	1916	1917	1918	1919
.350	.324	.377	.383	.420	.409	.390	.368	.369	.371	.383	.382	.384

COLORED CIRCLES REPRESENT A BATTING TITLE.

Cobb's base-stealing prowess is also well known and it's a measurable symbol of his reputation as the fiercest baserunner to play the game. Cobb led the majors in steals five times, only one fewer than Lou Brock and Rickey Henderson — not bad for one whose status as an original Hall of Famer would have been secure on his batting alone.

But this may surprise you. Because of his career batting average of .367, Cobb rarely is discussed as a power hitter. But over a 10-year period from 1907 to 1916, during which Cobb led the majors in batting average (.376) and stolen bases (624), he also

ranked seventh with 55 home runs.

To put that in the context of Cobb's era, note who ranked seventh in home runs over some other 10-year periods: Hank Greenberg in the 1930s, Vern Stephens in the '40s and Norm Cash in the '60s. Dave Kingman and Graig Nettles shared seventh in the 1970s; Tony Armas and Lance Parrish did so in the '80s. We'll discount Willie Mays as No. 7 in the 1950s because he would have ranked higher if he had not missed several years. That's OK — Ted Kluszewski ranked eighth.

By two other measures of power, ones that might have applied

more in Cobb's time than did home runs, Cobb ranks among the all-time best. He led the AL in total bases a league record six times, sharing that mark with Babe Ruth and Ted Williams. Cobb also led the league in extra-base hits three times, below Ruth's all-time high of seven titles, but equaling the totals of three sluggers from the live-ball era: Jimmie Foxx, Mickey Mantle and Albert Belle.

Cobb was clearly a "power hitter" for his time, whatever that may have been. Not bad, considering he also may have been the greatest batter and baserunner not only of his time, but of all-time.

LED THE LEAGUE IN STEALS 5 TIMES

1909	1911	1915	1916	1917
76	**83**	**96**	**68**	**55**
STOLEN BASES	STOLEN BASES	STOLEN BASES	STOLEN BASES	STOLEN BASES

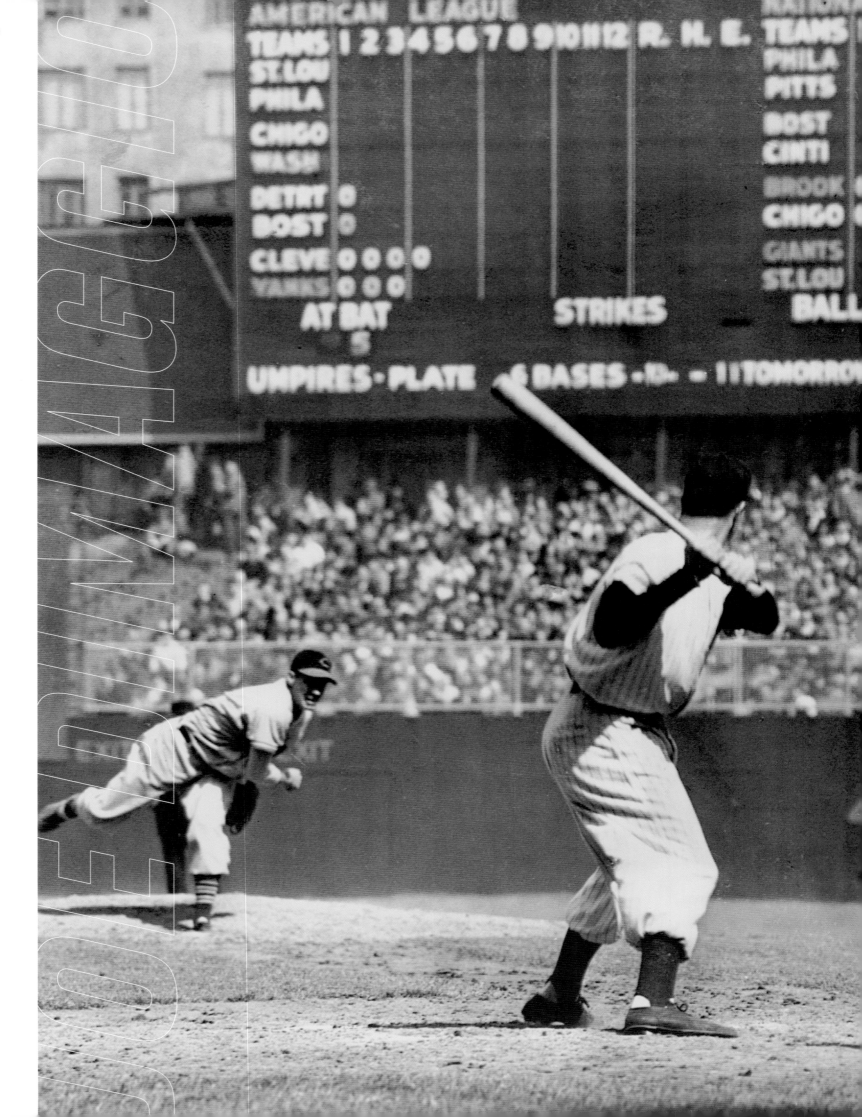

AMERICAN LEAGUE

TEAMS	1	2	3	4	5	6	7	8	9	10	11	12	R.	H.	E.
ST. LOU															
PHILA															
CHIGO															
WASH															
DETRT	0														
BOST	0														
CLEVE	0	0	0	0											
YANKS		0	0	0											

AT BAT   STRIKES   BALL
5

UMPIRES · PLATE   BASES   TOMORRO

TEAMS
PHILA
PITTS
BOST
CINTI
BROOK
CHIGO
GIANTS
ST. LOU

JUST AS LOU GEHRIG'S ASSOCIATION WITH HIS 2130-GAME PLAYING STREAK OBSCURED HIS OTHER ACCOMPLISHMENTS, SO DOES JOE DIMAGGIO'S 56-GAME HITTING STREAK MAKE IT EASY TO OVERLOOK HIS CAREER-LONG ACHIEVEMENTS. IN THE CASE OF DIMAGGIO, THERE ARE OTHER FACTORS THAT SERVED TO DIMINISH HIS STATISTICAL RECORD — THE PRIMARY MEANS BY WHICH CONTEMPORARY FANS MIGHT KNOW HIM — UNLESS ONE LOOKS BEYOND THE KIND OF STATISTICS THAT WOULD APPEAR ON THE BACK OF A BASEBALL CARD.

DIMAGGIO'S DAILY DOUBLE

Year	Runs	RBI
1936	132	125
1937	151	167
1938	129	140
1939	108	126
1940	93	133
1941	122	125
1942	123	114

It's safe to say DiMaggio's value wasn't overlooked by the managers or fans of his era. They made him one of only two players to be named to the All-Star team in every season of his career during which a game was played. (The other is Gehrig).

Over the first seven years of his career, DiMaggio led the majors in both RBIs and runs scored. Only four other players in this century did so in either category: Ralph Kiner, Ernie Banks, Johnny Bench and Don Mattingly in RBIs; Stan Musial, Mickey Mantle, Bobby Bonds and Rickey Henderson in runs. Gehrig, who ranked second in both categories over his first seven seasons, was the closest any player came to DiMaggio's extraordinary daily double.

MAJOR LEAGUE DEBUT 05/03/36 — WEIGHT 193 — HEIGHT 6'2" — THROWS R — BATS R — BIRTHPLACE MARTINEZ, CA — BORN 11/25/14 — PLAYER JOE DiMAGGIO

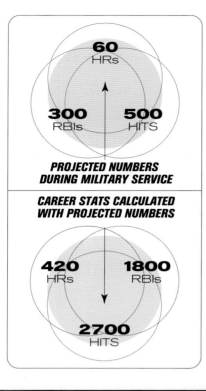

60
HRs

300
RBIs

500
HITS

*PROJECTED NUMBERS
DURING MILITARY SERVICE*

*CAREER STATS CALCULATED
WITH PROJECTED NUMBERS*

420
HRs

1800
RBIs

2700
HITS

1937
ALL-STAR GAME SLUGGERS
[FROM LEFT TO RIGHT]
**LOU GEHRIG, JOE CRONIN, BILL DICKEY, JOE DIMAGGIO,
CHARLIE GEHRINGER, JIMMIE FOXX, HANK GREENBERG.**

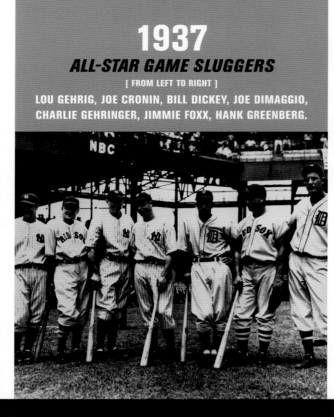

NUMBER OF SEASONS WITH MORE HOME RUNS THAN STRIKEOUTS

	PLAYER	BATS
7	JOE DIMAGGIO	R
6	YOGI BERRA	L
5	BILL DICKEY	L
5	TED KLUSZEWSKI	L
4	TOMMY HOLMES	L
4	ERNIE LOMBARDI	R
4	LEFTY O'DOUL	L
4	TED WILLIAMS	L
3	FRANK MCCORMICK	R
3	JOHNNY MIZE	L
3	KEN WILLIAMS	L

ALL-STAR
EVERY YEAR IN THE MAJORS
[THE ONLY OTHER PLAYER TO ACCOMPLISH THIS WAS LOU GEHRIG]

DiMaggio might have extended his leadership to eight seasons or more, perhaps even to his entire career. But near his peak, from the age of 28 to 30, DiMaggio missed three seasons in military service during World War II. Trying to estimate how much DiMaggio lost is tricky on account of his performance in 1942. Coming off three consecutive seasons with 30 or more home runs and batting averages above .350, did DiMaggio's totals of 21 homers, 114 RBIs and a .305 batting average in 1941 represent merely an "off year"? Or did they signal the start of a downturn that coincided with his military service — though one that still left him with credentials most other players would envy?

Whatever the answer, DiMaggio's performance in most of his six postwar seasons resembled that of 1942. But even at that level, it's clear DiMaggio sacrificed more than 60 home runs, 300 RBIs and 500 hits during his three lost seasons. That would have allowed him to retire with roughly 420 home runs and more than 1,800 RBIs and 2,700 hits.

DiMaggio wasn't robbed of more impressive credentials only by military service. No player's career home run total was compromised more by his home field

than was DiMaggio's by playing his home games at Yankee Stadium. In the *1991 Elias Baseball Analyst*, we estimated that before the elimination in 1976 of its distant fences in left-center field and the infamous "Death Valley", Yankee Stadium reduced home runs for right-handed hitters by approximately 37 percent.

The effect on DiMaggio was extreme. He hit 65 more home runs on the road (213) than he hit at home (148) — the largest such disparity in major league history. Incidentally, two other right-handed hitters for the Yankees rank among the top six in that category: Elston Howard ranks fourth (54 at home, 113 on the road) and Gil McDougald ranks sixth (29 at home, 83 on the road).

Ted Williams spoke with respect of DiMaggio and Willie Mays as the greatest hitters he has seen, but added the obvious — DiMaggio was by far the better at making contact. That is the crux of one of DiMaggio's most outstanding achievements. He had more home runs than strikeouts seven times in his career — not only the high for all batters during the live-ball era, but particularly impressive as a right-handed hitter. The significance is that during DiMaggio's career, three-quarters of all starting pitchers threw right-handed.

WILL IT BE BROKEN?

56-GAME

HITTING STREAK

Records are broken when conditions are favorable. For example, Roger Maris broke Babe Ruth's record of 60 home runs in 1961, when the league-wide average of one homer every 36 at-bats was an all-time high (to that point). Mark McGwire broke Maris' mark in 1998, when the rate of one HR every 33 ABs was the third-highest of all time.

With regard to DiMaggio's 56-game streak, this suggests two things: First, if batting averages rose to levels such as those, say, in the 1920s — when the major league average was in the .290s twice — the possibility that DiMaggio's mark would fall would be much greater than it is today. There is no reason that couldn't happen. If averages rose beyond that level, it might even be likely the record would be broken in time. But so what?

The fact is, it has been nearly six decades since the record was set.

Conditions during that time have remained relatively stable; league-wide batting averages have fallen within 10 points of the 1941 average (.262) 48 times in those 58 seasons. (And keep in mind that DiMaggio set the mark under somewhat unfavorable conditions: In 1941, the MLB average had fallen to .262, a 23-year low!) During that 58-year period, 12 of the 17 players who reached the 30-game mark failed to add even two more games to their streaks. Only Pete Rose came within 15 games of DiMaggio and none came within 10.

Perhaps nothing puts DiMaggio's record in context as well as the following table. It shows the players with the 10 highest batting averages over the period from 1941 through 1999 and indicates the longest hitting streak for each player during that time:

PLAYER	AVERAGE	STREAK	PLAYER	AVERAGE	STREAK
Ted Williams	.346	23	Rod Carew	.328	25
Tony Gwynn	.338	25	Frank Thomas	.321	21
Mike Piazza	.332	24	Edgar Martinez	.318	17
Stan Musial	.331	30	Kirby Puckett	.318	17
Wade Boggs	.328	28	Roberto Clemente	.317	20

NOT ONE PLAYER IN THAT GROUP HAD A BATTING STREAK LONGER THAN 30 GAMES AND ONLY MUSIAL AND BOGGS EXCEEDED EVEN THE 25-GAME MARK! DIMAGGIO'S HITTING STREAK IS THE DOMINANT BASEBALL RECORD OF THE SECOND HALF OF THE 20TH CENTURY, REGARDLESS OF WHETHER IT SURVIVES THE 21ST.

FROM THE TIME OF HIS MAJOR LEAGUE DEBUT IN 1989, KEN GRIFFEY JR. HAS FACED THE CHALLENGE OF GREAT POTENTIAL AND EXCEEDED LOFTY EXPECTATIONS.

KEN GRIFF

THE NEXT WILLIE MAYS?

(A) s the son of the most underrated member of the Big Red Machine, Junior quickly raised the bar well beyond the accomplishments of his dad, a three-time All-Star and career .296 hitter with 200 steals. As a 20-year-old sophomore, Junior hit 22 home runs to exceed his father's career high and he started a streak of five consecutive .300 seasons even Senior, a seven-time .300 hitter, never approached.

Junior even managed to satisfy those who labeled him the "next Willie Mays," surpassing many of the achievements of the man considered by some to have been the best all-around player of the century. With two weeks to go in the 1900s, Griffey, still not 30 years old, had as many MVP awards as Mays had won at that age (1), and more All-Star appearances (10 to 9), home run titles (3 to 1), and Gold Glove Awards (9 to 4) than Mays had earned at that point.

In fact, Griffey will hit more home runs by the age of 30 than any other player in major league history. The top six: Griffey, 395 as of age 29; Jimmie Foxx, 379; Mickey Mantle, 374; Eddie Mathews, 370; Mel Ott and Hank Aaron, 342. So heading into the new millennium, Griffey once again faces a challenge — in this case, the ultimate one: Can he break Aaron's record?

	WILLIE MAYS	KEN GRIFFEY JR.	
1	MVP Awards	1
1	Home Run Titles*	3
4	Gold Gloves*	9
9	All-Star Games	10

* Not including 1999 season

Although Junior has set the fastest first-half pace ever, he still needs roughly 350 home runs to surpass Aaron. Only three players have hit that many homers after age 30: Ruth (430), Aaron himself (413), and Mays (375). It doesn't take more than simple arithmetic to understand why: Ten years times 35 homers — a tough goal that only 13 other players have attained at any point in their careers — still equals only 350 home runs. Add another 50 as a high-end estimate of what he might hit after his 40th birthday. (Even in the era of the designated hitter, only three players topped the 50-mark: Carlton Fisk, 72; Darrell Evans, 60; and Dave Winfield, 59.) So unless Junior can do what only three players have done after the age of 30, and given the benefit of what only a handful have done after the age of 40, it will be difficult.

PLAYER	BORN	BIRTHPLACE	BATS	THROWS	HEIGHT	WEIGHT	MAJOR LEAGUE DEBUT
KEN GRIFFEY, JR.	11/21/69	DONORA, PA	L	L	6'3"	205	04/03/89

NUMBER OF HOME RUNS BY AGE 30

GRIFFEY	**395⁺**
FOXX	**379**
MANTLE	**374**
MATTHEWS	**370**
AARON, OTT	**342**

CAN HE BREAK AARON'S RECORD? IT WILL BE DIFFICULT.

One variable that many analysts and other fans will consider when guessing whether Griffey will surpass Aaron is his home ballpark. When the Mariners vacated the Kingdome in July 1999 and moved to Safeco Field, it immediately was judged a negative for Junior. But the fact is, although the Kingdome had a reputation as a great home run hitters' park, it was only moderately so.

It's true that there were a lot of home runs hit there — an average of 2.3 per game during the 1990s that ranked sixth among 29 ballparks used throughout most of the decade. But that was more on account of the Mariners players than their ballpark.

Griffey hasn't been Seattle's only longball threat for the past decade. Far from it, in fact. He and Jay Buhner became the first teammates since Willie Mays and Willie McCovey to play 10 seasons together and hit a total 600 home runs during that time. In the second half of the decade, the development of Edgar Martinez as a power hitter and the arrival of Alex Rodriguez created what may be the greatest quartet of home run hitters ever to play an extended period together. Their combined total of 535 home runs from 1995 through 1998 broke the previous four-year high of 498 set by Duke Snider, Gil Hodges, Roy Campanella and Carl Furillo of the Brooklyn Dodgers from 1953 through 1956. In 1998, they became the first group of four teammates ever to top the 600-HR mark over five seasons.

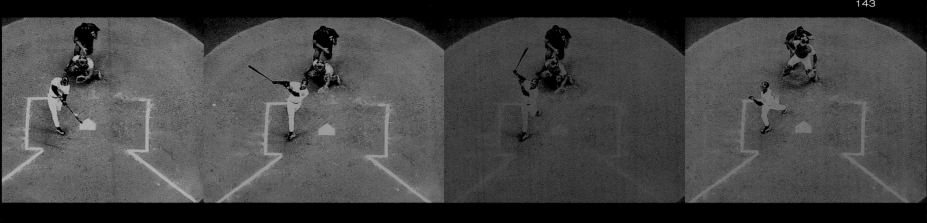

DURING GRIFFEY'S TENURE

| **HOME** [KINGDOME] | 1 HOME-RUN FOR EVERY **31.4** AT-BATS |
| **AWAY** [ROAD GAME] | 1 HOME-RUN FOR EVERY **32.5** AT-BATS |

During Griffey's tenure there, there was an average of one home run for every 31.4 at-bats at the Kingdome, compared to one every 32.5 ABs in Mariners road games. That would suggest the Kingdome increased home runs by approximately 3 percent.

Griffey himself hit 17 more home runs at the Kingdome (198) than he did on the road during the same period (181) — a slightly greater margin than would be expected from the stadium totals. But the point is that it's not such a large margin that Griffey should suffer significantly from leaving. An additional 17 home runs over 10 seasons would be the equivalent of missing, say, a half-season with an injury — not an unlikely event over a 10-year period, and one that Griffey has already encountered.

But the early returns on Safeco Field are not encouraging. Over the first month-and-a-half of play, there was an average of one home run per 33 at-bats at Safeco Field, well below the rates in Mariners 1999 road games (one per 26 AB) and earlier in the season at the Kingdom (one per 21).

Whatever Safeco's effect, it will probably be less than lots of other factors, many of which are unpredictable and some of which can't even be identified. Better, maybe, just to sit back and enjoy.

ROOKIE SEASON: BATTING AVERAGE .274 HOME RUNS 20 RUNS BATTED IN 68

WILLIE MAYS

L ike Joe DiMaggio and Jackie Robinson, Willie Mays had a career bookended by a pair of World Series appearances. Mays was a rookie on the Giants team that reached the 1951 Series on the strength of Bobby Thomson's "shot heard round the world". Twenty-two years later, Mays closed out his career with another World Series appearance, this one for the "Ya Gotta-Believe" Mets.

Ironically, Mays' teams blew leads to lose both of those World Series appearances. The Giants led the Yankees 2-games-to-1 in 1951 but lost in six games. The Mets took a 3-2 lead in 1973 before losing to the A's in seven. (Robinson's Dodgers also lost in his first and last World Series appearances, in 1947 and 1956.)

Mays' career was compromised after one of the most auspicious rookie seasons in major league history, when he missed most of the

1952 season and all of 1953 in military service. In 1951 Mays batted .274 with 20 home runs and 68 RBIs — numbers that seem much less than they actually are considering that Mays was 20 years old.

Mays is one of 110 rookies to hit 20 home runs or more, a group whose career paths run the gamut from Joe Charbonneau and Kevin Maas to Mark McGwire and Ted Williams. But only two rookies besides Mays did so before turning 21: Eddie Mathews (25) and Tony Conigliaro (24 at age 19); and only four other rookies posted between 15 and 19 homers at age 20 or younger: Johnny Bench, Ruben Sierra, Ken Griffey Jr. and Andruw Jones.

More than 300 players had more RBIs as rookies than Mays did (68). But only five of them were younger than 21: Phil Cavarretta (82), Johnny Bench (82), Andruw Jones (70), Hank Aaron (69) and Butch Wynegar (69). Note that every one of the 10 "young" rookies mentioned to this point was a multiple All-Star — with the exception of Andruw Jones, who eventually could be one. Mays, Aaron, Mathews and Bench are Hall of Famers; Tony C. might have been were it not for his beaning and Junior is likely to be.

PLAYER	BORN	BIRTHPLACE	BATS	THROWS	HEIGHT	WEIGHT	MAJOR LEAGUE DEBUT
WILLIE MAYS	05/06/31	WESTFIELD, AL	R	R	5'11"	180	05/25/51

IMAGINE WHAT MAYS MIGHT HAVE DONE IF HE HADN'T LOST TWO SEASONS TO THE MILITARY AFTER HIS ROOKIE SEASON. EDDIE MATHEWS AND TONY CONIGLIARO, THE ONLY OTHERS TO HIT 20 HOMERS AS ROOKIES BEFORE THE AGE OF 21, HIT 87 AND 60 RESPECTIVELY IN THEIR SECOND AND THIRD SEASONS COMBINED. HAD MAYS EVEN APPROACHED THOSE TOTALS IN 1952 AND 1953, IT WOULD HAVE BEEN HIS RECORD AARON WAS CHASING, NOT BABE RUTH'S.

Upon his return from military service, Mays became part of the legendary trio immortalized as Willie, Mickey and the Duke who all played center field for New York teams from 1954 to 1957. All three ranked in the major league top 10 in home runs in each of those seasons; and with one exception they ranked among the top 20 in RBIs in all four years. For the four-year period, they ranked 1-2-3 in home runs (Snider, 165; Mays, 163; Mantle and Eddie Mathews, 150); and all three ranked among the top seven in RBIs (Snider, 1st/459; Mantle, 5th/425; Mays, 7th/418). Note that it was Snider who posted the best offensive numbers during that period, surpassing those of his more heralded partners.

But what's most impressive about Mays' accomplishments during his tenure in New York is that they served as a prelude to what he achieved after the Giants moved to San Francisco. He batted .347 in his first season on the West Coast, then posted eight 100-RBI seasons from 1958 through 1966. That was the longest such streak during the second half of the century until matched by Frank Thomas 33 years later. Mays' five-year total of 226 homers from 1961 through 1965 was the third-highest in history. (Ralph Kiner hit 234 from 1947 to 1951 a record broken by Sammy Sosa in the final month of the 1999 season.) With a string of Gold Gloves dating from the award's inception in 1957 through 1968, there was little in the 1960s to dispel the widely held perception of Mays as the game's greatest active player.

Mays' career wound down in a fashion that almost guaranteed the glow of his accomplishments would fade. As his chances to catch Ruth's then-record total of 714 homers vanished in the late 1960s, Hank Aaron's ultimately successful pursuit gained steam. Mays' return to New York to finish his career with the Mets might have been a triumphant finale a couple years earlier, but at the age of 41 and 42, with his skills diminishing rapidly, Mays played 135 regular-season games over a year-and-a-half for the Mets with nearly as many strikeouts (90) as hits (96) during that time. He started only one of New York's 12 postseason games in 1973 — the opening game of the 1973 World Series — otherwise sitting in favor of Don Hahn.

For some time, Mays was the symbol of a player whom fans felt might have "held on" for too long. It's oddly ironic that those two seasons — at a time when few players remained active into their forties — could even impact one's image of Mays' storied career. More appropriate would be to imagine what Mays might have done had he not lost two seasons to the military following his rookie season. Eddie Mathews and Tony C., the only others to hit 20 homers as rookies before the age of 21, hit 87 and 60 respectively in their second and third seasons combined. Had Mays reached those totals in 1952 and 1953, it would have been his record that Aaron was chasing, not Babe Ruth's.

WAS HE THE GREATEST PLAYER EVER?

BABE

PLAYER	BORN	BIRTHPLACE	BATS	THROWS	HEIGHT	WEIGHT	MAJOR LEAGUE DEBUT
BABE RUTH	02/06/1895	BALTIMORE, MD	L	L	6'2"	215	07/11/14

RUTH

RUTH
AS A PITCHER
IN HIS FIRST THREE SEASONS

65	WINS
33	LOSSES

2:02 ERA

67	VICTORIES BY AGE
23	

ONLY THREE PITCHERS IN THIS
CENTURY WON MORE GAMES
THAN RUTH BY AGE 23:

BOB FELLER	107
SMOKY JOE WOOD	81
DWIGHT GOODEN	73

 ith both of his most hallowed records surpassed, Babe Ruth's accomplishments may seem less remarkable to future generations of fans as they did to those who watched those marks survive for decades. But Ruth's standing as the game's most dominant player and personality can't truly fade based on the achievements of players a half-century or more later. The fact is, Ruth attained that position by dominating his sport against his contemporaries in a way that only a few transcendent players — Chamberlain, Pele and Gretzky come to mind — did in their own sports.

Ruth's stats are still impressive, to say the least. More than 60 years after his retirement, he ranks second in major league history in home runs (714) and RBIs (2,212), and he's by far the all-time leader in slugging percentage (.690, compared to .634 by runner-up Ted Williams). But Ruth so dominated his time that when he set a record with 29 home runs in 1919, he hit more than the next two players combined (Gavvy Cravath, 12; and several others 10). And when he shattered his own mark with 54 homers a year later, he hit more than the next three (George Sisler, 19; Tilly Walker, 17; and Cy Williams, 15).

Try to imagine an analogous feat in any category in any current sport. Greg Maddux winning as many games as Roger Clemens, Tom Glavine, Pedro Martinez combined? Brett Favre throwing as many touchdown passes as Steve Young, Troy Aikman and Drew Bledsoe? Shaquille O'Neal scoring as many points as Karl Malone, Allen Iverson and Grant Hill? In the truest sense of the word, unbelievable. But that is how Ruth's performance must have appeared to opponents and fans in 1920.

At the time of his retirement, he had nine of the 15 highest single-season home-run totals in major league history. Through 1935, there had been only 24 seasons of 40 home runs or more — 11 by Ruth, a total of 13 by the other 6,409 players to appear in a major league game to that point.

Despite the fact that he batted in front of Lou Gehrig for most of his career, Ruth is also the all-time leader in walks (2,062). He led the majors 11 times; only two other players did so even half as often (Ted Williams seven times and Roy Thomas six times). The significance: Had Ruth walked as often as, say, the player who ranked 10th in the majors in each of those 11 seasons — still a considerable number of walks — it would have provided him with an additional 699 at-bats. Considering his home run rates in those seasons, that would have translated into 67 more home runs.

Clearly those accomplishments present a compelling case for Ruth as the greatest hitter who ever lived. But there can be no argument that he was the greatest *player* ever, based on one simple fact: Given a chance, Ruth might have become one of the game's great pitchers. Consider that in his first three seasons, before he began the transition to outfielder, Ruth posted a record of 65-33 with a 2.02 ERA. The ERA was the fourth best in the majors during those three seasons (1915-1917) and he ranked third in victories during that span behind a pair of high-end Hall of Famers, Grover Cleveland Alexander (94-35) and Walter Johnson (75-49).

By the time he turned 23, Ruth had earned 67 victories. Only three pitchers in this century won more games by that age: Bob Feller (107), Smoky Joe Wood (81) and Dwight Gooden (73).

Generations later, it's difficult to appreciate the magnitude of Ruth's unprecedented hitting achievements, at least as they were viewed by his contemporaries. Perhaps only in recent years, as Mark McGwire stretched the limits of what many once considered possible, have we seen anything to help put Ruth in that context. But combined with what Ruth did as a pitcher, and the unrealized potential that it implied, there really is nothing before or after to compare.

THERE CAN BE NO ARGUMENT THAT RUTH WAS THE GREATEST *PLAYER* EVER, BASED ON ONE SIMPLE FACT: GIVEN A CHANCE, RUTH ALSO MIGHT HAVE BECOME ONE OF THE GAME'S GREAT PITCHERS.

TED WILLIAMS

50/50
PROPOSITION

AS THE ALL-TIME LEADER WITH AN ON-BASE PERCENTAGE OF .482, TED WILLIAMS EMBODIED EVERYTHING THAT MANAGERS VALUE IN A PLAYER. WILLIAMS MADE OUTS LESS FREQUENTLY THAN ANY OTHER PLAYER IN MAJOR LEAGUE HISTORY. ONLY ONE OTHER PLAYER, BABE RUTH, HAD A MARK ABOVE .450. (RUTH'S WAS .474.)

It often is noted even great hitters make out seven times out of 10. Not always true. With Williams, it was nearly a 50/50 proposition. Consider this: From 1941, when he became the last .400 hitter, to 1954, Williams posted a major league best .351 batting average. He also led the majors in walks in each of the eight seasons during that period in which he played at least 100 games. (He missed much of the 1950 season with an injury suffered in the All-Star Game and he missed most or all of five others during that time in military service.) Williams' on-base percentage during the 14-year span: .497!

Williams's batting eye is legendary and it's supported by his career average of 2.8 walks for every strikeout. There have been a few others with higher marks during the live-ball era — 12, to be exact — but none who even approached the power of Williams. Players who rank high in that category are generally high-contact singles hitters, guys like Frankie Frisch, Paul Waner and Nellie Fox. In fact, among the top 30 in walk-to-strikeout ratio during the live-ball era, ranging from leader Joe Sewell (7.4) to Bill Dickey (2.3), none had a home-run rate even half as high as did Williams, who averaged one homer every 14.8 at-bats. Williams combined hitting, selectivity and power to a greater degree than any other player in history.

So many stars of the 1940s served in the military that it's tempting to lump them together with regard to time lost and its effect on their careers. Williams, Joe DiMaggio, Dom DiMaggio, Tommy Henrich, Johnny Mize, Pee Wee Reese, Phil Rizzuto and Enos Slaughter were among the several dozen established players who missed the 1943, 1944 and 1945 seasons in their entirety. But it's possible that no one lost as much as Williams, who for starters was the only one of the above to serve in Korea as well. (He played a total of 43 games in 1952 and 1953.)

MAJOR LEAGUE DEBUT	04/20/39
WEIGHT	205
HEIGHT	6'3"
THROWS	R
BATS	L
BIRTHPLACE	SAN DIEGO, CA
BORN	08/30/18
PLAYER	TED WILLIAMS

Using New Age tools to estimate how much Williams might have lost during his military service is as illuminating as it is fun. Step 1 is to find players with the most similar statistical profile to Williams'. Step 2 is to use their future performance as a basis from which to estimate what Williams might have done. In order, the five most similar players were:

STEP 1

PLAYER	YEAR	BA	HR	RBI	CAREER TOTALS	BA	HR	RBI
LOU GEHRIG	1928:	.374	27	142	THROUGH 1928:	.343	111	511
JOE DIMAGGIO	1939:	.381	30	126	THROUGH 1939:	.341	137	558
CHUCK KLEIN	1931:	.337	31	121	THROUGH 1931:	.360	125	470
JOHNNY MIZE	1939:	.349	28	108	THROUGH 1939:	.346	99	416
FRANK THOMAS	1994:	.353	38	101	THROUGH 1994:	.326	142	484
TED WILLIAMS	1942:	.356	36	137	THROUGH 1942:	.356	127	515

The actual calculations were based on a wider range of statistics that also included walks and strikeouts, extra-base hits and stolen bases. But the statistics above indicate the basics. Other players who contributed (in lesser proportion) to the estimate of what Williams would have accomplished from 1943 to 1945 were Hank Greenberg, Jimmie Foxx, Hal Trosky and Mickey Mantle.

When the numbers were crunched, then adjusted for the ways in which Williams differed from the group averages, the three-year estimate for Williams was:

STEP 2

	G	AB	R	H	2B	3B	HR	RBI	BB	SO	BA
1943 TO 1945	463	1,753	521	628	129	30	136	514	667	132	.358

The same process was used to estimate what Williams would have done during the two seasons he barely played on account of service in Korea (1952-1953). Some of the same players served as "models"— Foxx (through 1940), Gehrig (through 1935) and Mantle (through 1965), along with a number of others (Mel Ott, Stan Musial and Frank Robinson among them). The results:

STEP 3

	G	AB	R	H	2B	3B	HR	RBI	BB	SO	BA
1952 TO 1953	312	1,145	253	376	69	15	69	273	251	117	.328

Now comes the amazing part. By "restoring" what Williams lost during those periods, we can construct new career totals:

	G	AB	R	H	2B
ACTUAL	2,292	7,706	1,798	2,654	525
ADJUSTED	3,024	10,503	2,553	3,617	717

THOSE ADJUSTED TOTALS WOULD HAVE PUT WILLIAMS ATOP THE ALL-TIME LISTS BY WIDE MARGINS IN RUNS SCORED (HIS ACTUAL RANK IS 14TH), RBIs (11TH), EXTRA-BASE HITS (11TH) AND BASES ON BALLS (2ND). HE WOULD HAVE RANKED THIRD IN HOME RUNS – THOUGH WITH 712, IT'S POSSIBLE HE WOULD HAVE PLAYED ANOTHER SEASON TO BREAK RUTH'S MARK, ULTIMATELY GIVING HANK AARON A HIGHER TARGET AT WHICH TO SHOOT.

WILLIAMS' GOAL WASN'T TO HIT .400, IT WAS TO BE A .400 HITTER.

Those adjusted totals would have put Williams atop the all-time lists by wide margins in runs scored (his actual rank is 14th), RBIs (11th), extra-base hits (11th) and bases on balls (2nd). He would have ranked third in home runs—though with 712, it's possible he would have played another season to break Ruth's mark, ultimately giving Hank Aaron a higher target at which to shoot.

So much for conjecture. We've filled the page and still not mentioned the number .406, Williams' batting average in 1941 when he became the last .400 hitter. It stands by itself, not requiring any statistical ornamentation. (For the record, Williams' .551 on-base percentage in '41 might be the more amazing achievement, though it lacks the sexiness of a .400-plus batting average.) But it's worth noting that in his quest for the .400 mark that season, Williams reached the final day with a mark of .39955 — a cosmetic .400 average when rounded off that might have satisfied the fans and the media, but not one that would have suited either the statisticians or the player himself.

So Williams played, both games of a doubleheader in fact, against a pair of left-handers he never had faced before. He went six-for-eight, not only validating his status as a true .400 hitter but also making a statement about the nature of a champion. Williams later said that he played those final games and took those final swings because if he hadn't it "wouldn't have been honest." He recognized a .400 average was supposed to be the measure of an accomplishment, not just a goal in itself. Williams' goal wasn't to hit .400, it was to be a .400 hitter. There have been none since.

3B	HR	RBI	BB	SO	BA
71	521	1,839	2,019	709	.344
115	712	2,589	2,916	946	.344

BEFORE THE 1985 SEASON, PETE ROSE WAS ASKED HOW MANY AT-BATS HE THOUGHT IT WOULD TAKE TO GET THE 94 HITS HE NEEDED TO EQUAL TY COBB'S LONGSTANDING RECORD OF 4191 CAREER HITS. ROSE REPORTEDLY REPLIED, "NINETY-FOUR." SUCH POSITIVE THINKING MIGHT BE LAUGHABLE WERE IT NOT FOR ROSE'S MANY ACCOMPLISHMENTS, ESPECIALLY BREAKING COBB'S MARK — EVEN IF IT DID TAKE HIM 256 MORE AT-BATS THAN HE PREDICTED HE WOULD NEED TO BREAK THE RECORD.

PETE ROSE

We're not sure when Rose first "decided" he would mount a successful assault on Stan Musial's National League record for hits (3,630), then on the 4,000-hit mark, and eventually on the record that Cobb had held since 1923. But it's important to understand that even in 1971, when Rose turned 30 with a total of 1,540 hits, it must have seemed a longshot to everyone other than Rose himself and his legion of fans.

Even though Rose already had posted five 200-hit seasons by that time, leading the majors in hits three times, there were 36 players in major league history who had more hits at the same age. Not only would Rose be chasing Musial's and Cobb's records; he already had spotted a lead to them and to 34 other pretty fair hitters. At age 30, he was 2,651 hits short of Cobb's record — a total that's three fewer than Ted Williams amassed in his entire career. Any other player might have been daunted; but to Pete, who expected no less than a hit in every at-bat, it was a wholly attainable goal.

By the time Rose turned 35, he had added two more hits titles — again leading the majors both times — and 1,018 more hits. In real terms, Rose now was starting to bear down on Musial's NL mark. More significantly, there were now only 11 players who had set a faster pace, with more hits than Rose at the time of their 35th birthdays.

When Rose turned 40 in April 1981, he had Musial in his sights. Rose's hit count had reached 3,565, just 65 short of Stan the Man's mark. Through durability and consistency, Rose had now passed most of the rest of field. Only one player had more hits by age 40 — Cobb himself. Still, Rose was a 40-year-old player with little speed, even less power, and diminishing defensive skills. He was also 626 hits short of the record.

It was at this point that an evolving change in the nature of records, and of players' attitudes toward them, became crucial to Rose's challenge of Cobb's mark. With more players remaining active into their 40s and teams playing longer schedules, older records of long standing were starting to topple with regularity. Ruth's home run mark was gone, as

PLAYER	BORN	BIRTHPLACE	BATS	THROWS	HEIGHT	WEIGHT	MAJOR LEAGUE DEBUT
PETE ROSE	04/14/41	CINCINNATI, OH	B	R	5'11"	200	04/08/63

was Cobb's stolen base record. Walter Johnson's strikeout mark was about to fall. Gehrig still looked safe, but guess who made his major league debut on the very night that Rose broke Musial's record?

Along with the higher salaries that gave a great incentive for players to extend their careers, ever stronger athletes of increasing skill now had another advantage in chasing hallowed records. With the publication of breakthrough books such as *The Baseball Encyclopedia* in 1969, and a press and broadcasting corps that had grown increasingly enamored of statistics, fans and players alike paid more attention than ever to

records to chase or feats to achieve. Players also were willing to make sacrifices to attain them. No better example exists than that of Jerry Reuss, who won more than 200 games over more than 20 years as a highly regarded major league pitcher, but nevertheless spent much of the 1990 season laboring in the minors. His goal: to face even a single major-league batter in 1990 and thereby become a "four-decade player." (He had made his major league debut in 1969.) Reuss became one of only 22 players in major league history to do so, with another group eligible in the 2000 season.

ROSE AT 30

3 HIT TITLES

CHASING 34 OTHER HITTERS IN PURSUIT OF TY COBB

1971

1540

TOTAL HITS TO DATE

1972
ROSE WINS FOURTH HIT TITLE
SEASON TOTAL:
198
CAREER TOTAL:
1738

1973
ROSE WINS FIFTH HIT TITLE
SEASON TOTAL:
230
CAREER TOTAL:
1968

1976
ROSE WINS SIXTH HIT TITLE
SEASON TOTAL:
215
CAREER TOTAL:
2578

1977
ROSE HAS 44-GAME HIT STREAK
CAREER TOTAL:
2776

In Rose's case, he had a target and it was one that may have become an obsession if only because it had taken so much time and talent to get even within several hundred hits of Cobb. That target gave Rose a goal to focus on and a reason to keep playing. That's the pursuer's advantage: He knows how far he has to go. Cobb had no such goal to keep him active and swinging beyond the point at which he ceased to be a useful player. He didn't set out to reach 4,191; that just happened to be the number on the counter when it stopped spinning. Yet it became a magical

goal for those in pursuit — something real at which to aim.

Beyond his extraordinary hitting ability, unsurpassed determination and a measurable, identifiable goal, Rose had one other advantage — one that eventually may have provided the winning edge in his pursuit of Cobb's record. With his career as a useful player fading — done, some would say — Rose was traded back to the Cincinnati Reds, mired in fifth place and eager to add a drawing card. Cincinnati's manager was happy to put Rose's name in the lineup on a regular basis, something that Bill Virdon was reluctant to do with the Expos before the trade and which Phillies manager Paul Owens declined to do in two of the last three games of the previous season's World Series. Of course, that accommodating skipper was Rose himself, hired in August 1984 to be Cincinnati's player-manager.

Despite the fact Rose failed to hit a single home run in either 1983 or 1984, Manager Rose gave himself 119 starts at first base in 178 games between the time he was hired and when he broke Cobb's record. While his .288 batting average looks respectable, Rose's slugging percentage for

that period (.356) wasn't even that of a typical starting second baseman (.368), let alone that of a first baseman (.436), a traditional "power position." He hit just two home runs with 53 RBIs during that time; a typical first baseman, given 119 starts, would have batted .275 and provided 15 home runs and 64 RBIs.

On September 11, 1985, Rose broke the record.

With or without the record, Rose's career was studded with great achievements. He won three batting titles and he won MVP awards for both a regular season (1973) and a World Series (1975). His 44-game

1985
ON SEPTEMBER 11
ROSE BREAKS TY COBBS
HIT RECORD.
4192

1984
ROSE BECOMES
CINNCINNATI REDS
PLAYER/MANAGER
CAREER HIT TOTAL:
3872

1981
ROSE WINS
SIXTH
HIT TITLE
SEASON TOTAL:
140
CAREER TOTAL:
3507

1986
4256
TOTAL CAREER
HITS

ROSE FINISHES A
24-YEAR CAREER WITH
THREE BATTING TITLES,
SIX HITTING TITLES,
A REGULAR SEASON
MVP IN 1973, A
WORLD SERIES MVP IN
1975 AND A RECORD
10 SEASONS WITH
200+ HITS.

hitting streak in 1977 is the longest since DiMaggio's 56-game streak. Rose set an all-time record for 200-hit seasons with 10, one more than Cobb. He tied Cobb's mark of leading the majors in hits seven times and he led the NL nine times in reaching base (hits plus walks plus hit-by-pitch), a league record. He also led the league in doubles five times. Those were all important to Rose, who often said he wanted to lead the league in hits, walks, and doubles, because those were individual

But in the end, Rose's playing career will be defined by the most important record he set — career hits. It's ironic and fitting that this record, more than any of his others, is a testament to determination and durability as well as talent, all of which contributed to his selection to the All-Century Team. And true to Rose's controversial nature, it's a lightning rod to those who feel he compromised his team's chances by focusing on a purely personal goal.

YEAR	LEAGUE	PLAYER	AVG.	HR	RBI
1922	NL	Rogers Hornsby	.401	42	152
1925	NL	Rogers Hornsby*	.403	39	143
1933	AL	Jimmie Foxx	.356	48	163
1933	NL	Chuck Klein	.368	28	120
1934	AL	Lou Gehrig*	.363	49	165
1937	NL	Joe Medwick	.374	31	154
1942	AL	Ted Williams*	.356	36	137
1947	AL	Ted Williams	.343	32	114
1956	AL	Mickey Mantle*	.353	52	130
1966	AL	Frank Robinson	.316	49	122
1967	AL	Carl Yastrzemski	.326	44	121

ickey Mantle won the American League Triple Crown in 1956 with a .353 batting average, 52 home runs and 130 RBIs — an across-the-board performance that ranks as one of the greatest seasons in major league history. There have been 11 Triple Crown seasons during the live-ball era. Mantle is one of four players who won what we might call the "Major League Triple Crown," leading all players in both leagues in all three categories. Those players are indicated by asterisks in the accompanying table.

There now has been an entire generation of baseball fans who never have witnessed a Triple Crown season. Since Yastrzemski became the last winner in 1967, only one player has finished even among the top two in his league in all three categories: Jeff Bagwell, who did it in the strike-shortened 1994 season. There are few certainties about what would have happened over the final two months of the '94 season. But one thing is for sure: Bagwell would not have challenged for a Triple Crown. He broke a bone in his left hand when hit by a pitch on the next-to-last day of play.

Popular opinion, not the least of which was the player's own frequent and touching admissions, holds that Mantle would have accomplished much more if he had taken better care of himself.

But no one makes the All-Century Team on the basis of what he might have done. Mantle's actual achievements were still remarkable: the last MLB-wide Triple Crown; named to 20 All-Star teams (including 13 starts); four home-run titles; and three Most Valuable Player awards. He hit 18 World Series home runs in 65 games, a record on the short list of those unlikely ever to be broken. At the time of his retirement, Mantle ranked third in major league history with 536 home runs, trailing only Babe Ruth and Willie Mays.

PLAYER	BORN	BIRTHPLACE	BATS	THROWS	HEIGHT	WEIGHT	MAJOR LEAGUE DEBUT
MICKEY MANTLE	10/20/31	SPAVINAW, OK	B	R	5'11"	198	04/17/51

Mantle also had great speed. His stolen base totals aren't impressive by today's standards — 153 for his career and only one season with 20 or more. They reflect the era and the fact the Yankees were built around power. But Mantle ranked in the AL's top 10 in steals for six straight seasons from 1955 to 1960. And his combination of power and speed was so unusual that over a period of 10 years, from 1953 to 1962, no American League player had more homers and more steals than Mantle in the same season.

As for what Mantle lost to injuries and destructive self-indulgence, we only can guess. But it wouldn't be much of a stretch to consider Ken Griffey Jr. to be the second coming of Mantle and use the second half of Junior's career as an indication of what The Mick might have done. The statistical similarity over their first eight seasons — each compared to the other at the same age — is stunning:

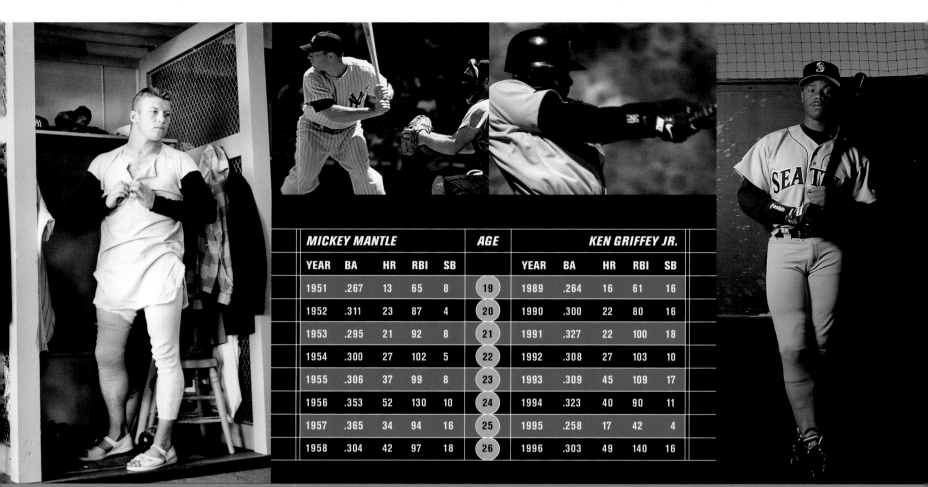

MICKEY MANTLE					AGE	KEN GRIFFEY JR.				
YEAR	BA	HR	RBI	SB		YEAR	BA	HR	RBI	SB
1951	.267	13	65	8	19	1989	.264	16	61	16
1952	.311	23	87	4	20	1990	.300	22	80	16
1953	.295	21	92	8	21	1991	.327	22	100	18
1954	.300	27	102	5	22	1992	.308	27	103	10
1955	.306	37	99	8	23	1993	.309	45	109	17
1956	.353	52	130	10	24	1994	.323	40	90	11
1957	.365	34	94	16	25	1995	.258	17	42	4
1958	.304	42	97	18	26	1996	.303	49	140	16

IN 1961, WHEN ROGER MARIS BROKE BABE RUTH'S SINGLE-SEASON HOME-RUN RECORD, HE DID NOT RECEIVE A SINGLE INTENTIONAL WALK. THAT'S BECAUSE MANTLE WAS BATTING BEHIND HIM FOR MOST OF THE SEASON

If Griffey's 1994 season is pro-rated to account for the games lost to the strike, his projected totals of 58 HR and 130 RBI are comparable to even Mantle's in his Triple Crown season. The only poor match during the eight years above would be at age 25, when Griffey missed more than half the season with a broken wrist. Double his home-run and RBI totals for that season and once again they virtually match Mantle's.

Perhaps there's no statistic that illustrates the respect opposing teams had for Mantle better than this one: In 1961, when Roger Maris broke Babe Ruth's single-season home run record, he did not receive a single intentional walk. That's because Mantle was batting behind him about 80 percent of Maris' plate appearances. Maris' home-run rate in '61 was nearly twice as high with Mantle on-deck (one every 8.8 at-bats) as

it was with others batting behind him (one per 16.4 ABs). Maris' batting average was more than 100 points higher when he batted in front of Mantle that season (.293) than it was with others on-deck (.174).

Incidentally, since intentional walks were first compiled on an official basis in 1955, more than 200 players have hit 40 homers in a season. Only two didn't draw an intentional walk: Maris in 1961 and Alex Rodriguez in 1998. Rodriguez batted second in Seattle's lineup, right in front of Griffey.

Unique among the elite company represented by this squad, Mickey Mantle's actual accomplishments whet the appetite for what he might have done had he remained healthy enough long enough to reach his full potential. As we've suggested here, to estimate the heights he should have reached, keep an eye on Junior.

MANTLE WAS ONLY 24 YEARS OLD WHEN HE WON HIS TRIPLE CROWN IN 1956 — THE ONLY SEASON, INCIDENTALLY, IN WHICH HE LED THE AL IN EITHER BATTING AVERAGE OR RBIS. AT SUCH A YOUNG AGE — ONLY WILLIAMS WAS YOUNGER WHEN HE WON HIS FIRST TRIPLE CROWN — MANTLE'S POTENTIAL SEEMED LIMITLESS.

STAN MUSIAL

TO BASEBALL FANS OF THE POSTWAR ERA, A DISCUSSION OF WHO WAS THE GAME'S GREATEST HITTER OFTEN INCLUDED ONLY TWO NAMES: TED WILLIAMS AND STAN MUSIAL. THROUGHOUT THE 1960S AND 1970S, THERE SEEMED ABOUT EQUAL SUPPORT FOR BOTH HALL OF FAMERS. BUT IT SEEMS WILLIAMS HAS HAD A MUCH BETTER LAST 20 YEARS BECAUSE AS APPRECIATION FOR HIS ACCOMPLISHMENTS HAS GROWN, MUSIAL'S STAR HAS WANED. IT IS NO LONGER COMMON TO HEAR MUSIAL MENTIONED AS THE GREATEST HITTER OF HIS TIME, AT LEAST OUTSIDE ST. LOUIS.

That seems an odd statement to make of a seven-time batting champ, who was the all-time National League leader in runs, hits and RBIs at the time of his retirement. But you wouldn't necessarily glean that by checking his page in the Baseball Encyclopedia. The batting titles are obvious from the boldface type in the batting-average column. But there are few such clues in those other "scoreboard" categories.

For instance, even though Musial was the NL leader in career RBIs until passed by Hank Aaron in 1971, he led the league only twice. The fact that he ranked in the league's top eight every season from 1943 to 1957 (except for 1945 when he was in military service) speaks volumes about both his productivity and consistency. It's the longest such streak in the live-ball era. But it doesn't earn him any boldface type — the unmistakable mark of a league leader.

Now let's raise the stakes, from RBIs to home runs. There the difference between Musial's "boldface quotient" and his year-in, year-out productivity is even more extreme: His career total of 475 home runs is the highest in major league history among players who never led their league.

A triple is one of the most exciting plays in baseball, but do many fans know from day to day or from year to year who leads the league? Do they even care? Regardless, that's the category in which Musial led the NL a record five times. In fact, his career total of 177 ranks second during the live-ball era to Paul Waner's (190).

Even more impressive is the fact Musial led the majors in the more encompassing category of extra-base hits seven times, an all-time high. Only four other players in this century did so even half as often as Musial: Babe Ruth (six times), Hank Aaron, Ernie Banks and Hank Greenberg (four times each). So why doesn't that earn Musial some boldface recognition? Because no popular reference book, baseball card or other source of statistical information has a column for extra-base hits. He did earn some serious boldface by leading the NL in doubles eight times from 1943 to 1954. But that category lacks the significance of extra-base hits or the cachet of batting average, homers or RBIs. Nevertheless, extra-base power is one of the main reasons why so many of those who saw Musial play considered him the game's greatest hitter.

POSTWAR ERA'S GREATEST HITTER?

PLAYER	BORN	BIRTHPLACE	BATS	THROWS	HEIGHT	WEIGHT	MAJOR LEAGUE DEBUT
STAN MUSIAL	11/21/20	DONORA, PA	L	L	6'	175	09/17/41

7

TIME NATIONAL LEAGUE BATTING CHAMPION

1942	.315
1943	.357
1944	.347
1946	.365
1947	.312
1948	.376
1949	.338
1950	.346
1951	.355
1952	.336
1953	.337
1954	.330
1955	.319
1956	.310
1957	.351
1958	.337
1959	.255
1960	.275
1961	.288
1962	.330
1963	.255
TOTAL	**.331**

RBI LEADER

Musial was the NL leader
in career RBIs until passed
by Hank Aaron in 1971.
He led the league only twice.

475 HOME RUNS

His career total of 475 home
runs is the highest in major
league history among players
who never led their league.

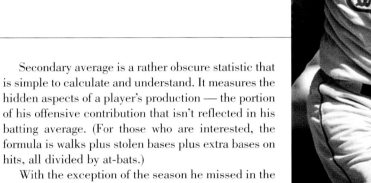

18.3 STRIKEOUTS PER PLATE APPEARANCE

Among the top 200 home
run hitters, only Joe DiMaggio
and Yogi Berra had lower
strikeout rates than Musial.

EXTRA BASE HITS — 7-TIME LEADER

Musial led the majors
in extra-base
hits seven times, an
all-time high.

Secondary average is a rather obscure statistic that is simple to calculate and understand. It measures the hidden aspects of a player's production — the portion of his offensive contribution that isn't reflected in his batting average. (For those who are interested, the formula is walks plus stolen bases plus extra bases on hits, all divided by at-bats.)

With the exception of the season he missed in the military, Musial ranked in the NL top 10 in secondary average every season over a 20-year period from 1943 through 1962. That would be spectacular even for a player with a low batting average. Remember, that's what this statistic is designed for:

To measure the contribution not included in a batting average. But Musial perennially placed among the leaders in secondary average in addition to being a seven-time batting champ whose batting average ranked among the league's top five in 17 of those 20 seasons — including every season in which he played from 1942 to 1958!

It's worth noting also that among the top 200 home run hitters in major league history, only Joe DiMaggio and Yogi Berra had lower strikeout rates than Musial, who struck out once per 18.3 plate appearances.

WHEN A GROUP OF 260 WRITERS, BROADCASTERS, OWNERS, PLAYERS AND UMPIRES VOTED IN 1956 FOR THE BEST PLAYER OF THE DECADE (THE FIRST 10 SEASONS AFTER THE END OF WORLD WAR II), MUSIAL WAS THE WINNER, GAINING 14 MORE FIRST-PLACE VOTES THAN RUNNER-UP JOE DIMAGGIO AND NEARLY TWICE AS MANY AS WILLIAMS.

WOULD HE WIN SUCH A POLL TODAY?

IT MAY BE THAT AS GREAT AS HIS RECORD IS, MUSIAL WAS A PLAYER WHO HAD TO BE SEEN TO BE APPRECIATED FULLY.

★

ALEXANDER, GROVER C. [1911–1930] (R)
BROWN, MORDECAI [1903–1916] (R)
CARLTON, STEVE [1965–1988] (L)
CLEMENS, ROGER [1984–PRESENT] (R)
DEAN, DIZZY [1930–1941,47] (R)
ECKERSLEY, DENNIS [1975–1998] (R)
FELLER, BOB [1936–1956] (R)
FINGERS, ROLLIE [1968–1985] (R)
FORD, WHITEY [1950–1967] (L)
GIBSON, BOB [1959–1975] (R)
GROVE, LEFTY [1925–1941] (L)
HUBBELL, CARL [1928–1943] (L)
JOHNSON, WALTER [1907–1927] (R)
KOUFAX, SANDY [1955–1966] (L)
MADDUX, GREG [1986–PRESENT] (R)
MARICHAL, JUAN [1960–1975] (R)
MATHEWSON, CHRISTY [1900–1916] (R)
PAIGE, SATCHEL [1948–1953,65] (R)
PALMER, JIM [1965–1984] (R)
PLANK, EDDIE [1901–1917] (L)
ROBERTS, ROBIN [1948–1966] (R)
RYAN, NOLAN [1966–1993] (R)
SEAVER, TOM [1967–1986] (R)
SPAHN, WARREN [1942–1965] (L)
WALSH, ED [1904–1917] (R)
YOUNG, CY [1890–1911] (R)

(R) = RIGHT-HANDED
(L) = LEFT-HANDED

★

PITCHER

ALL-CENTURY TEAM PITCHER ★ ALL-CENTURY TEAM PITCHER ★ ALL-CENTURY TEAM PITCHER ★ ALL-CENTURY TEAM PITCHER ★

AT THE AGE OF 30, ROGER CLEMENS APPEARED DESTINED FOR THE KIND
OF GREATNESS HIS SELECTION TO THE ALL-CENTURY TEAM SUGGESTS.
HE ALREADY HAD ASSEMBLED A COLLECTION OF HONORS THAT INCLUDED
FOUR ERA TITLES AND THREE CY YOUNG AWARDS.

t that point, Clemens suffered a mediocre span of four seasons during which he posted a 40-39 record. The Boston Red Sox surely didn't think a turnaround was just ahead. With Clemens' contract expired, they offered him a new deal commensurate more with the pitcher who ranked 43rd in victories over the previous four seasons than with one who had won four ERA titles. After all, so had Walter Johnson. But in the winter of 1996, Clemens' best years seemed as much like ancient history as Johnson's did.

Clemens rebounded with not only the two best seasons of his career, but arguably the best back-to-back seasons of any American League pitcher in the second half of the 20th century. He led the league in victories, ERA, and strikeouts — the so-called "pitcher's triple crown" — in both seasons. The last pitcher to win a triple crown had been Dwight

Gooden in 1985; the last AL pitcher was Hal Newhouser (1945); and the last AL pitcher to do so in consecutive seasons was Lefty Grove (1930-1931).

(It should be noted the Red Sox rebounded from their questionable call on Clemens by signing 1997 NL Cy Young award winner Pedro Martinez, who promptly posted two Clemens-like seasons in Boston. In fact, as the 1999 season headed into its final two weeks, Martinez was poised to win a triple crown of his own.)

In 1998, Clemens launched a streak of 20 consecutive decisions without a loss, an AL record, and his streak of 30 consecutive starts without a loss was the longest in the majors in this century. In addition to winning his fifth and sixth ERA titles, he won two more Cy Young Awards, becoming the only pitcher to win as many as five.

Ks

ERA   WINS

97|98

BACK-TO-BACK SEASONS

PITCHING TRIPLE CROWN

ROGER CLEMENS

PLAYER	BORN	BIRTHPLACE	BATS	THROWS	HEIGHT	WEIGHT	MAJOR LEAGUE DEBUT
ROGER CLEMENS	08/04/62	DAYTON, OH	R	R	6'4"	220	05/15/84

Only Grove has won more ERA titles than Clemens. The leaders: Grove, 9; Clemens, 6; Grover Alexander and Sandy Koufax, 5; Walter Johnson and Greg Maddux, 4. Those numbers shouldn't be glossed over. Only two ERA titles are up for grabs each year, no exceptions. To put Clemens' total in perspective, he has won as many as Nolan Ryan, Jim Palmer, Bob Gibson, and Bob Feller combined. In fact, there are 15 pitchers in the Hall of Fame who spent the majority of their careers in the live-ball era who never won an ERA title, including Dizzy Dean, Robin Roberts, Ferguson Jenkins and Gaylord Perry. For emphasis: Clemens has won six. So far.

Clemens' continued mastery 15 years after his debut puts him in elite company on that count as well. He won his first ERA title in 1986, his most recent in 1998. Only four pitchers won them at least 10 years apart: Warren Spahn, 14 (1947-1961); Grove, 13 (1926-1939); Clemens, 12 (1986-1998); and Walter Johnson, 11 (1913-1924).

ERA TITLES

9	LEFTY GROVE
6	ROGER CLEMENS
5	GROVER ALEXANDER
5	SANDY KOUFAX
4	WALTER JOHNSON
4	GREG MADDOX

The similarities between Clemens and Grove run beyond the ones noted above. They are the only Red Sox pitchers to win more than one ERA title, doing so in Fenway Park, a hitters' park. They also won their ERA titles during the greatest hitters' eras of the century. Perhaps this explains in part why Grove could be the best pitcher not voted by fans to the All-Century Team and it suggests Clemens may seem less to future generations than we know him to be today.

Actually, some fans came a bit late to their appreciation of Clemens. He was part of an exceptional class of rookie pitchers in 1984, which included Dwight Gooden and Bret Saberhagen. In 1985, Gooden captured national attention with one of the greatest seasons ever by a pitcher (at age 20); and Saberhagen won a Cy Young award and the World Series MVP. But Clemens was limited to 15 starts by a shoulder injury that eventually required surgery. Even when Clemens rebounded from the surgery in 1986 with a spectacular 24-4 season, it didn't seem quite so extraordinary after what Gooden had done a year earlier.

When Gooden and Saberhagen faltered in the late 1980s, Clemens still wasn't viewed by some as the best pitcher in the game. Orel Hershiser won the same awards as Saberhagen — Cy Young and Series MVP — in 1988 and he broke a high-profile record for consecutive scoreless innings. But in the end, he couldn't match Clemens' ongoing record of excellence either.

Clemens did what great players do: He compiled a record that went beyond a great accomplishment or two and beyond just a couple years. He was the first pitcher since Juan Marichal to start his career with nine consecutive winning seasons. His outstanding seasons in 1997 and 1998 raised Clemens to an even higher plane. His selection to the All-Century Team signifies he is now compared not to the best of his era, but to the best of all time.

ROGER CLEMENS HAS WON AS MANY ERA TITLES AS NOLAN RYAN, JIM PALMER, BOB GIBSON AND BOB FELLER COMBINED.

BOB GIBSON

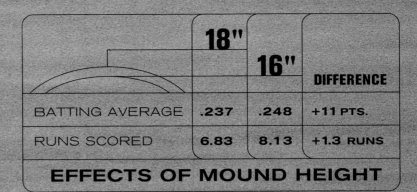

	18"	16"	DIFFERENCE
BATTING AVERAGE	.237	.248	+11 PTS.
RUNS SCORED	6.83	8.13	+1.3 RUNS

EFFECTS OF MOUND HEIGHT

RARELY DOES AN ATHLETE SO DOMINATE THE OPPOSITION THAT A RULE CHANGE IS REQUIRED TO LEVEL THE FIELD.

One example was the NCAA's no-dunk rule, implemented in 1967 to negate the superiority of Lew Alcindor. The rule was rescinded in 1976, by which time Alcindor had changed his name, graduated to the NBA and perfected his Sky Hook.

Changes that were similar in spirit followed the 1968 baseball season when pitchers so dominated the game the rules-makers determined hitters needed their help. The league-wide batting average in 1968 was .237, which remains the lowest in major league history. The average of 6.83 runs per game is the second lowest ever, fractionally higher than the 6.77 mark set in 1908. Baseball reacted by lowering the pitcher's mound and shrinking the strike zone. Batting averages increased by 11 points and scoring by 1.3 runs per game the next season.

Bob Gibson posted an ERA so low that even today it seems to have come from the previous century. Gibson's 1.12 ERA is an all-time National League record and it is the lowest mark of the live-ball era by a wide margin over the runner-up (Dwight Gooden's 1.53 mark in 1985). It boils down to this: He made 34 starts and allowed 38 earned runs.

Despite nine losses, Gibson's 1968 season deserves consideration as the greatest ever by a pitcher. For the season, he posted a 22-9 record, completing 28 of his 34 starts and throwing 13 complete-game shutouts. During one remarkable three-month period, Gibson pitched 12 shutouts over a span of 18 starts and won 15 consecutive decisions. Incidentally, he allowed more than three runs in only two of those losses and he twice lost games 1-0.

Gibson's ERA was spectacular not only by comparison to the 1968 National League average (2.99). It was extraordinary even by comparison to the other best pitchers in his own league. Gibson's ERA was 49 percent lower than the composite of the rest of the NL's top 10 in ERA (2.21) — a group that included four other Hall of Fame pitchers: Don Drysdale, Tom Seaver, Juan Marichal and Gaylord Perry. No other ERA leader in the live-ball era was so far superior to the rest of his league's top 10.

PLAYER	BORN	BIRTHPLACE	BATS	THROWS	HEIGHT	WEIGHT	MAJOR LEAGUE DEBUT
BOB GIBSON	11/09/35	OMAHA, NE	R	R	6'1.5"	195	04/15/59

DESPITE NINE LOSSES, GIBSON'S 1968 SEASON DESERVES CONSIDERATION AS THE GREATEST EVER BY A PITCHER.

Gibson was also one of the best postseason pitchers ever, if not the very best. His World Series record was 7-2, but even that barely suggests why such a small subset of his career — just nine postseason starts — so greatly impacts how Gibson is viewed and contributes so mightily to his selection to the All-Century Team.

Gibson pitched in an era when the World Series was the entire baseball postseason. Today's postseason builds interest and tension as storylines play out over a month-long elimination tournament. In the World Series of Gibson's era — with a maximum of just seven games deciding the world championship — each game had great intensity, like a short series of Super Bowls, Indy 500s or heavyweight championship fights would. As that era drew to a close, Gibson was its dominant player.

One cannot overestimate the attention focused on each of Gibson's nine World Series starts. He appeared in three World Series — 1964, 1967, and 1968 — and started Game 7 in each of them. No other pitcher started more than two seventh games in World Series competition. In 1964, his Game 7 victory marked the end of the Yankees dynasty. In 1967, he shattered the Red Sox' Impossible Dream. In 1968, he segued from his extraordinary regular-season performance into the World Series with a record-setting 17-strikeout victory over the Tigers. Four days later he defeated the Tigers again, winning his seventh consecutive postseason start — still a record, and all of them complete-game victories.

Gibson's sharp control could account in part for his lower HBP totals. But on that basis, Gibson ranks even lower. Over the last 60 years, there were more than 150 pitchers whose rate of HBPs per walk were higher than Gibson's (one HBP per 13.1 BBs). The highest rate belongs to Mike Smithson (one per 5.2); another intimidator, Don Drysdale, ranks second (5.6). Drysdale once hit Willie Stargell with a pitch after being ordered by manager Walter Alston to walk him intentionally. Drysdale's explanation: "Why waste three pitches?"

Gibson's low HBP total, especially relative to his reputation, is perhaps the best embodiment of true intimidation; existing more in the mind of the victim than in fact.

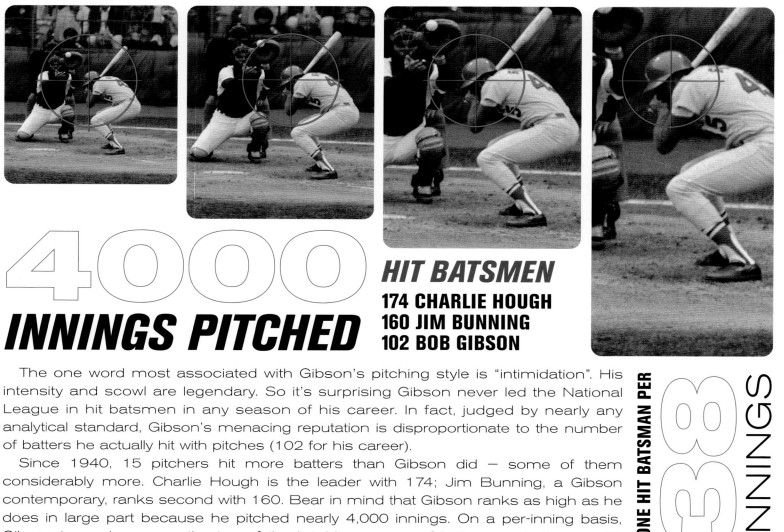

4000
INNINGS PITCHED

HIT BATSMEN
174 CHARLIE HOUGH
160 JIM BUNNING
102 BOB GIBSON

ONE HIT BATSMAN PER 38 INNINGS

The one word most associated with Gibson's pitching style is "intimidation". His intensity and scowl are legendary. So it's surprising Gibson never led the National League in hit batsmen in any season of his career. In fact, judged by nearly any analytical standard, Gibson's menacing reputation is disproportionate to the number of batters he actually hit with pitches (102 for his career).

Since 1940, 15 pitchers hit more batters than Gibson did — some of them considerably more. Charlie Hough is the leader with 174; Jim Bunning, a Gibson contemporary, ranks second with 160. Bear in mind that Gibson ranks as high as he does in large part because he pitched nearly 4,000 innings. On a per-inning basis, Gibson is nowhere near the top of the list. His average of hitting one batter per 38 innings is not even among the top 100 pitchers since 1940 (minimum: 1000 innings).

NOLAN RYAN

5,714 TOTAL STRIKEOUTS, 2,465 STRIKEOUTS AFTER AGE 35

ate in his career, Nolan Ryan was a frequent subject of talk-show debates — did he or didn't he belong in the Hall of Fame? This was long after it became apparent Ryan would be baseball's all-time strikeout king, even after he seemed likely to attain the 300-victory total commonly (though mistakenly) referred to as an "automatic" qualifier.

To be sure, Ryan's first-ballot election to the Hall's Class of 1999 provided a dramatic and decisive answer, and it demonstrated how underappreciated his accomplishments were for much of his career. But it also highlighted the extraordinary success Ryan had late in his career, turning critics and fence-sitters into admiring supporters. A dazzling fact to illustrate that point: Ryan struck out 2,465 batters after turning 35, more than Sandy Koufax, Juan Marichal or Jim Palmer did in their entire careers.

PLAYER	BORN	BIRTHPLACE	BATS	THROWS	HEIGHT	WEIGHT	MAJOR LEAGUE DEBUT
NOLAN RYAN	01/31/47	REFUGIO, TX	R	R	6'2"	195	09/11/66

The outcome of Ryan's battle in the mid-1980s with Steve Carlton for the strikeout crown was another example of his nearly unprecedented late-career success. In 1983, both pitchers approached Walter Johnson's record — a mark that had stood for more than six decades. Carlton had whittled Ryan's lead over him from a high of 269 strikeouts in 1979 to just 29 strikeouts when Ryan broke the record on April 27, 1983. A week later, Ryan was placed on the disabled list and within days of his return in early June, Carlton moved past him. That's right: Ryan broke a mark that had stood for 62 years, but owned it for only 41 days.

That was the first of 13 lead changes over a seven-week period. At one point, the lead changed with every appearance by either pitcher for eight starts in a row. But late in the 1983 season, when Carlton finally opened a lead that couldn't be erased in a good start or two, it was widely expected he steadily would draw away from Ryan. Although Lefty was two years older, he had won more games than Ryan in every season since 1975; his 15-16 mark in 1983 seemed only a slight blip after going 60-24 in the previous three seasons.

As it turned out, it was the other way around: Ryan had a decade of

good pitching left and Carlton was nearing the end of a great career. Ryan passed Carlton forever on September 5, 1984. Then he struck out another 1,852 batters compared to 279 for Carlton. Ryan earned 93 more victories, Carlton just 18.

His election to the Hall of Fame and the All-Century team aside, there always may be lingering debate as to whether Ryan was one of the greatest pitchers of all time. But there can be little question he was one of the toughest, if not the toughest, to hit. In the battle between batter and pitcher, a hit represents victory for the batter; a strikeout is the ultimate victory for the pitcher.

On both counts, Ryan is the hands-down champion. His total of 5,714 strikeouts is so far above that of the runner-up — Carlton with 4,136 — that it would take the seven best seasons of third-ranked Bert Blyleven to close the gap. His total of seven no-hitters equals those of the next two pitchers combined: Sandy Koufax had four, Bob Feller had three (and no one else in this century has more than two).

Let's combine the two measures. Only a few starting pitchers each season have more strikeouts than hits allowed. There was an average of

RYAN BROKE A RECORD THAT STOOD FOR 62 YEARS, AND HELD IT FOR 41 DAYS.

NUMBER OF SEASONS WITH MORE STRIKEOUTS THAN HITS ALLOWED
AMONG PITCHERS WITH AT LEAST 20 STARTS

CY YOUNG / CHRISTY MATHEWSON / GROVER CLEVELAND ALEXANDER / GAYLORD PERRY / WARREN SPAHN / ROBIN ROBERTS / EARLY WYNN — 0

JUAN MARICHAL — 1

DON DRYSDALE — 2

WALTER JOHNSON — 3

five per season during the 1970s (among pitchers with at least 20 starts); six during the 1980s; nine in the 1990s. Ryan had more strikeouts than hits allowed in every season of his career except two, including 21 in which he made at least 20 starts.

Only one other starting pitcher has had even half as many such seasons: Roger Clemens (11). Cy Young never had such a season, nor did Christy Mathewson or Grover Cleveland Alexander. Gaylord Perry never had one and neither did Warren Spahn, Robin Roberts or Early Wynn. Juan Marichal did it once, Don Drysdale did it twice. Walter Johnson, the strikeout king for 62 years, did it three times. Bob Feller, often considered the hardest thrower of all-time, did it four times. Sandy Koufax did it eight times and Tom Seaver nine, a total approached only by a handful of contemporary pitchers, including David Cone and Randy Johnson. For emphasis: Nolan Ryan did it 21 times.

Ryan's career ratio of 1.46 strikeouts per hit allowed is the second-highest in major league history (minimum: 100 starts). He trails only Randy Johnson (1.55). And there should be no doubt about the importance of strikeouts to a pitcher. When judging a pitcher's ability, a strikeout is not "just another out" — a once-popular myth that may have contributed to some fans' perception of Ryan as nothing more than a Hall of Fame contender.

The higher the strikeout rate, the more likely it is that a pitcher will have a winning record. Among pitchers whose career rates are between 5.00 and 5.99 strikeouts per nine innings, 61 percent had winning records. That percentage increases at each level: 68 percent had winning record among pitchers with rates from 6.00 to 6.99; 87 percent from 7.00 to 7.99; and 100 percent (12 of 12) with rates of 8.00 or higher.

For much of his career Ryan was dismissed as a ".500 pitcher" — simply not true. What Ryan didn't win was a Cy Young Award; and his only World Series ring was won in 1969, as a role player for the New York Mets. (Interesting fact: Ryan earned a save in his only appearance in a World Series game.) But by using the same analytical tool detailed in the Walter Johnson section, we can estimate Ryan added 82 victories to his teams, the 14th-highest total in this century.

For the record, the top 19 pitchers in that category include 18 Hall of Famers and Roger Clemens. Case closed.

DESPITE 27 YEARS IN THE MAJORS, RYAN DIDN'T WIN A CY YOUNG AWARD.

4	8	9	11	21
BOB FELLER	SANDY KOUFAX	TOM SEAVER	ROGER CLEMENS	NOLAN RYAN

WALTER JOHNSON

THE NUMBERS SUGGEST WALTER JOHNSON MIGHT HAVE BEEN THE MOST VALUABLE PITCHER OF THE CENTURY. THEN AGAIN...

Johnson was the all-time strikeout king for 62 years. He passed Cy Young in 1921 and extended his record by another 710 strikeouts over the next seven years. Johnson remained the leader until 1983, when Nolan Ryan and Steve Carlton traded the mark back and forth several times before Ryan claimed it for himself. If he still holds the mark in the year 2046, Ryan will have been the leader for as long as Johnson was.

Babe Ruth held the career home-run record long enough for 714 to become synonymous with "the unattainable" — for 53 years to be exact, nearly a decade shorter than Johnson held the strikeout mark. In fact, Johnson held the strikeout mark for the same number of years that Lou Gehrig held the record for consecutive games played. So even though his numbers have been smashed by Ryan, and surpassed by an ever-growing number of contemporary pitchers, Johnson's reign as strikeout king must be respected.

He led the majors in strikeouts seven times and there's a harmony in that total that helps put Johnson's career in perspective. Two pitchers share that record with Johnson: Bob Feller and Nolan Ryan each led the majors seven times. Each was considered the hardest-throwing, toughest-to-hit pitcher of his era. Many of today's fans saw Ryan pitch and heard of or know of Feller's accomplishments and reputation. Johnson was their patriarch.

JOHNSON WAS THE ALL-TIME STRIKEOUT KING FOR 62 YEARS.

PLAYER	BORN	BIRTHPLACE	BATS	THROWS	HEIGHT	WEIGHT	MAJOR LEAGUE DEBUT
WALTER JOHNSON	11/06/1887	HUMBOLDT, KS	R	R	6'1"	200	08/02/07

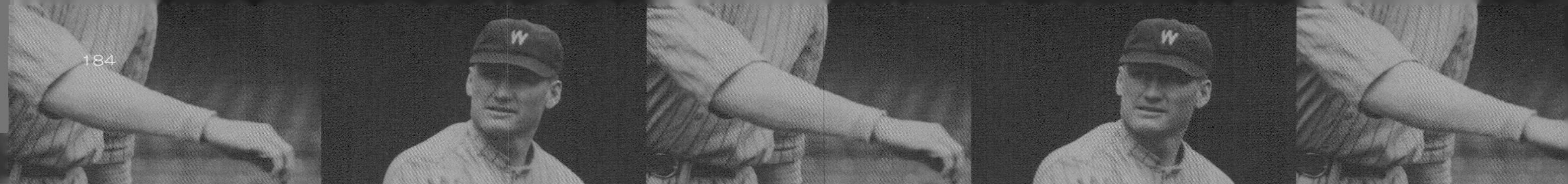

IS THE MOST VALUABLE PITCHER OF THE 20TH

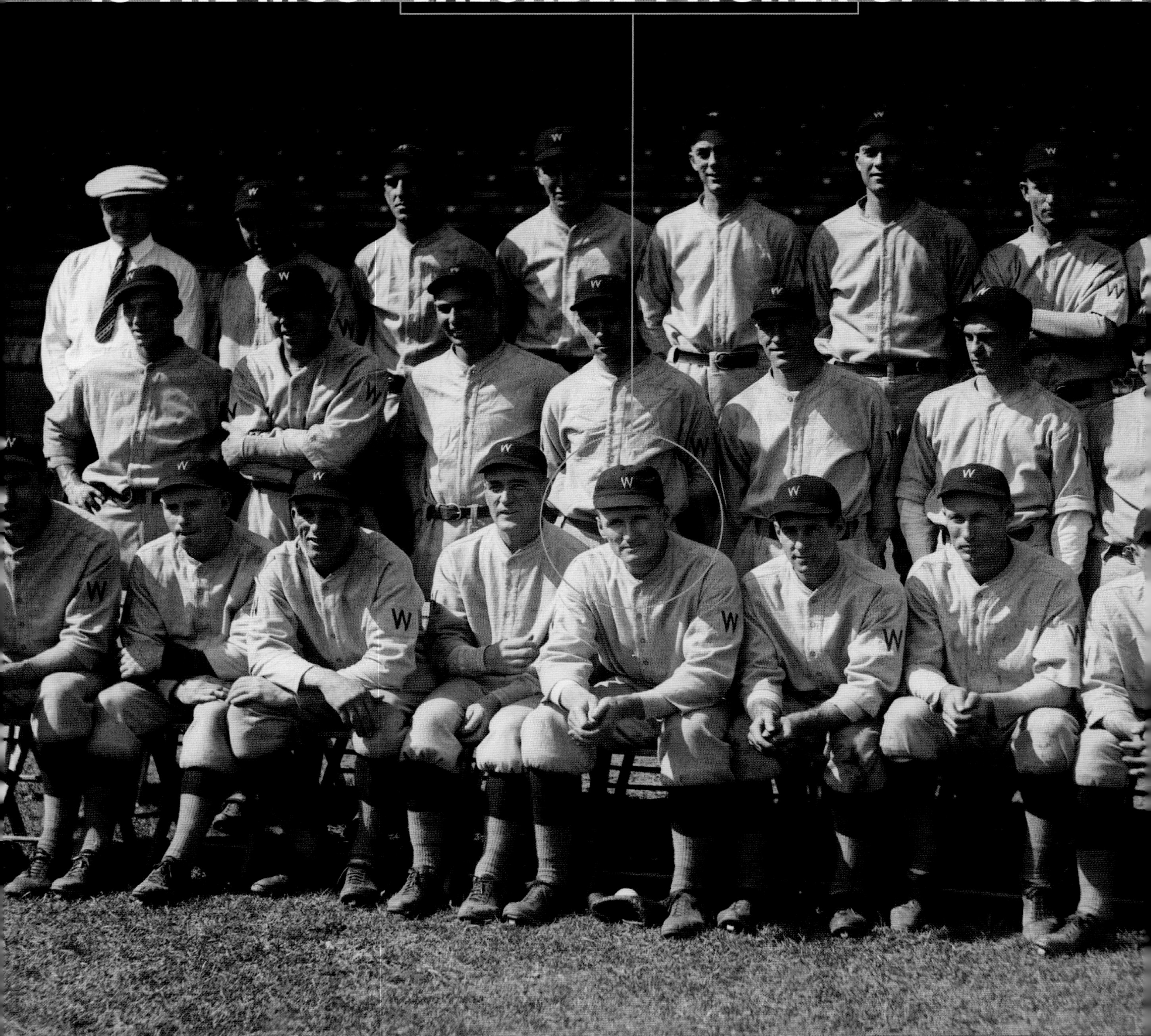

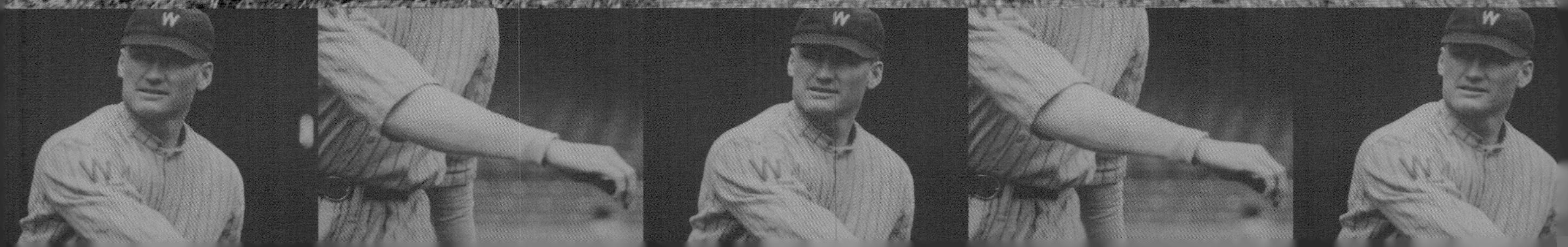

CENTURY A SIMPLE MATTER? WELL, YES AND NO.

In 1991, the Elias Sports Bureau introduced a technique for measuring the number of victories a starting pitcher was worth. The theory was simple: A pitcher's value to his team was defined as the difference between the number of games he won and the number that would have been won by whomever would have pitched in his place had he not been there. That makes as much sense to us today as it did when we first advanced the method nearly a decade ago. And before we know how many games each pitcher won in his career, the only tricky part is measuring how many games that theoretical "replacement pitcher" would have won.

The replacements are assumed to have a .400 winning percentage. Over the past 20 years, that's the median percentage of the pitchers in each season who made the sixth-most starts on each team — that is, the first replacement for the five members of the starting rotation. The specifics of how to estimate the number of games a .400 pitcher would have won for a given team are too technical and tedious to detail here.

But we performed that calculation for every pitcher in every season of this century, accounting for the number of starts and quality of the team. The last item is important: A theoretical .400 pitcher would have a much higher mark pitching for the 1998 Yankees (.613), a much lower one pitching for the 1962 Mets (.182).

When each pitcher's total victories were compared to the number that his replacements would have won, the largest gap belonged to Walter Johnson. Johnson had a record of 417-279 (.599). It was estimated that a pitcher with a .400 mark for typical teams would have posted a record of 254-442 (.365) making those starts for the teams for which Johnson pitched. (Johnson spent his entire 21-year career with the Washington Senators, who had a .462 winning percentage when he didn't earn a decision.)

The following table shows the top 10 for the century. Note that only seasons during the 1900s are included:

PITCHER	ACTUAL RECORD		REPLACEMENT RECORD		DIFF.
	W-L	PCT	W-L	PCT	
Walter Johnson	417-279	.599	254-442	.365	+163
Cy Young	438-275	.614	288-425	.404	+150
Grover Alexander	373-208	.642	232-349	.400	+141
Christy Mathewson	373-188	.665	260-301	.463	+113
Tom Seaver	311-205	.603	199-317	.386	+112
Warren Spahn	363-245	.597	259-349	.426	+104
Phil Niekro	318-274	.537	221-371	.373	+97
Lefty Grove	300-141	.680	204-237	.462	+96
Roger Clemens	245-130	.653	149-226	.397	+96
Steve Carlton	329-244	.574	237-336	.414	+92

So does this settle the matter? Although we have an awful lot of faith in this method, it shouldn't settle any arguments. Rather, it should be the starting point for debate. As well as the technique measures one specific and significant thing, it measures only that.

To understand much of what's missing, look no further than Sandy Koufax. Some say that from 1963 through 1966, Koufax may have had the best four-year period of any pitcher in history.

Using the same method as above to determine each pitcher's best four-year span, and then comparing them on that basis, moves Koufax from No. 69 in the century — a ranking unfairly compromised by his early retirement at the peak of his career — to fifth place.

But note who still ranks first on such a list:

PITCHER	YEAR	DIFF.	PLAYER	YEAR	DIFF.
Walter Johnson	1910-13	+61	Lefty Grove	1930-33	+43
Grover Alexander	1914-17	+52	Robin Roberts	1952-55	+40
Cy Young	1900-03	+47	Bob Feller	1940-46	+39
Christy Mathewson	1907-10	+46	Dazzy Vance	1922-25	+39
Sandy Koufax	1963-66	+44	Juan Marichal	1963-66	+38

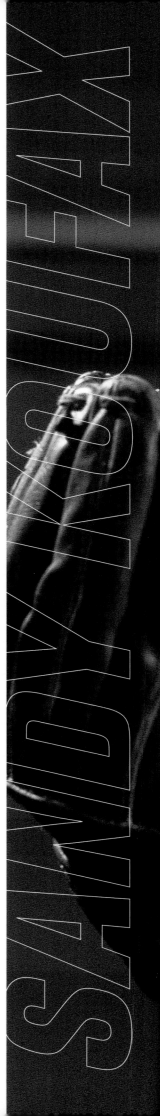

NO STAR IN THE BASEBALL GALAXY BLAZED BRIGHTER OR DISAPPEARED MORE SUDDENLY THAN SANDY KOUFAX.

A .500 pitcher for the first seven seasons of his career, Koufax gave a hint of what was to come in 1962: In his first season at Dodger Stadium, he posted a 14-7 record and sliced nearly a run off his ERA of the previous season, leading the National League with a 2.54 mark. Then, starting in 1963, Koufax strung together what may have been the best four-year stretch by any pitcher in major league history.

There is no formal Triple Crown for pitchers as there is for batters. But it seems reasonable that such a feat would consist of leading his league in victories, earned-run average, and strikeouts. That has become a fairly uncommon feat: Before Roger Clemens led the American League in all three categories in both 1997 and 1998, only one pitcher had done so in the previous 20 years — Dwight Gooden in 1985.

PLAYER	BORN	BIRTHPLACE	BATS	THROWS	HEIGHT	WEIGHT	MAJOR LEAGUE DEBUT
SANDY KOUFAX	12/30/35	BROOKLYN, NY	R	L	6'2"	210	06/24/55

PITCHING TRIPLE CROWN

FOUR GREATEST SEASONS EVER?

KOUFAX LED THE MAJOR LEAGUE IN	1963	1964*	1965	1966
WINS	⚾		⚾	⚾
ERA	⚾	⚾	⚾	⚾
SOs	⚾		⚾	⚾
		★ BECAUSE OF INJURIES, KOUFAX MISSES 12 STARTS		

Koufax not only led the NL in victories, ERA and strikeouts in 1963, he became the first pitcher to lead the majors in all three since Hal Newhouser in 1945. Then Koufax did it again in 1965 and in 1966. In 1964, injuries caused him to miss a dozen starts. He still pitched 223 innings and led the league in ERA and shutouts. Only six other pitchers in this century won this "Major League Triple Crown" even once: Grover Cleveland Alexander (1915), Walter Johnson (1913 and 1918), Dazzy Vance (1924), Lefty Grove (1930 and 1931), Newhouser (1945), and Gooden (1985).

Throughout that period, Koufax was the closest thing to an unhittable pitcher most fans ever had seen. When he struck out 306 batters in 1963, he became only the second pitcher since a young Walter Johnson to reach the 300-mark. Bob Feller had done so once, in 1946. Two years later, Koufax set a modern record with a previously inconceivable total of 382 strikeouts. Keep in mind that from 1937 to 1957, only one

National League pitcher reached even the 200-mark, and just barely at that. Johnny Vander Meer fanned 202 batters in 1942.

Koufax also tossed no-hitters in four consecutive seasons from 1962 to 1965. To put that in perspective, think of it this way: Only three other pitchers in this century pitched no-hitters in consecutive seasons: Warren Spahn (1960-1961), Nolan Ryan (1973-1974-1975) and Steve Busby (1973-1974). Koufax did it twice — and he put those pairs of seasons back-to-back. The only pitcher to throw more no-hitters overall was Ryan (7).

Koufax was rewarded with Cy Young awards in each of his Triple Crown seasons — he was the unanimous choice each time — he won an MVP award in 1963 and he finished a close second to Roberto Clemente in 1966. He also won the World Series MVP award twice, in 1963 and 1965 for winning two games in each of those Series. Koufax posted a 0.95 ERA in World Series play (57 innings).

382 STRIKEOUTS

4 NO-HITTERS

1965

1962   1963   1965
1964

And then, just like that, it was over. For years, Koufax had battled degenerative arthritis in his left elbow with ice, diathermy, anti-inflammation medication and, eventually, cortisone shots. But when he announced the condition was forcing him to retire, it made little sense to those who had watched his extraordinary work over the previous four seasons, culminating in what might have been the best of them.

No other pitcher in this century retired coming off a 20-victory season; Koufax won 27 in 1966. None retired following a 200-strikeout season; Koufax struck out 317 in 1966. No pitcher since Koufax has retired after placing in his league's top 10 in ERA. Koufax did so after leading the majors by a quarter-run per nine innings, his league by a half-run, with a 1.73 mark.

To be sure, Koufax wasn't the first pitcher whose career ended prematurely because of injury, nor was he the last. Dizzy Dean, Don Gullett, J.R. Richard and Smokey Joe Wood, to name a few, could have supplemented an all-world rotation with Koufax. But for one thing, Koufax never would have allowed that. A five-man rotation? Even when doctors warned him that pitching every fourth day would hasten his retirement, he made 40 or more starts in three of his last four seasons. And with no disrespect intended to those other pitchers, Koufax wasn't just a good pitcher, or — dare we say — even just a great pitcher.

He was one for the ages. He wasn't forced to retire merely a couple years early; he retired at the age of 30, losing as much as a decade or more. And he did so at a time when he was redefining the meaning of "peak of his career," accomplishing things never done before. Only eight other pitchers in the 1900s won 78 of 100 decisions at any point in their careers. Koufax won 78 of his *last* 100 decisions. Just as Koufax's future seemed limitless, the future was over.

3 CY YOUNG AWARDS   0.95 WORLD SERIES ERA

1963
1965
1966

1963
1965

CY YOUNG

MANY OF TODAY'S BASEBALL FANS KNOW CY YOUNG MORE FOR THE AWARD
NAMED IN HIS HONOR THAN FOR HIS ACCOMPLISHMENTS. SOME FANS
ARE FAMILIAR WITH THE FACT YOUNG IS, BY FAR, THE ALL-TIME LEADER IN
VICTORIES WITH 511, HIS DEFINING RECORD. BUT DID YOU KNOW, FOR
INSTANCE, THAT IF THEY NAMED AN AWARD FOR THE PITCHER WHO LOST THE
MOST GAMES, THAT ALSO WOULD BE CALLED "THE CY YOUNG AWARD?".
THAT'S RIGHT — YOUNG ALSO LOST MORE GAMES THAN ANYONE ELSE (314).

PLAYER	BORN	BIRTHPLACE	BATS	THROWS	HEIGHT	WEIGHT	MAJOR LEAGUE DEBUT
CY YOUNG	03/29/1867	GILMORE, OHIO	R	R	6'2"	210	08/06/1890

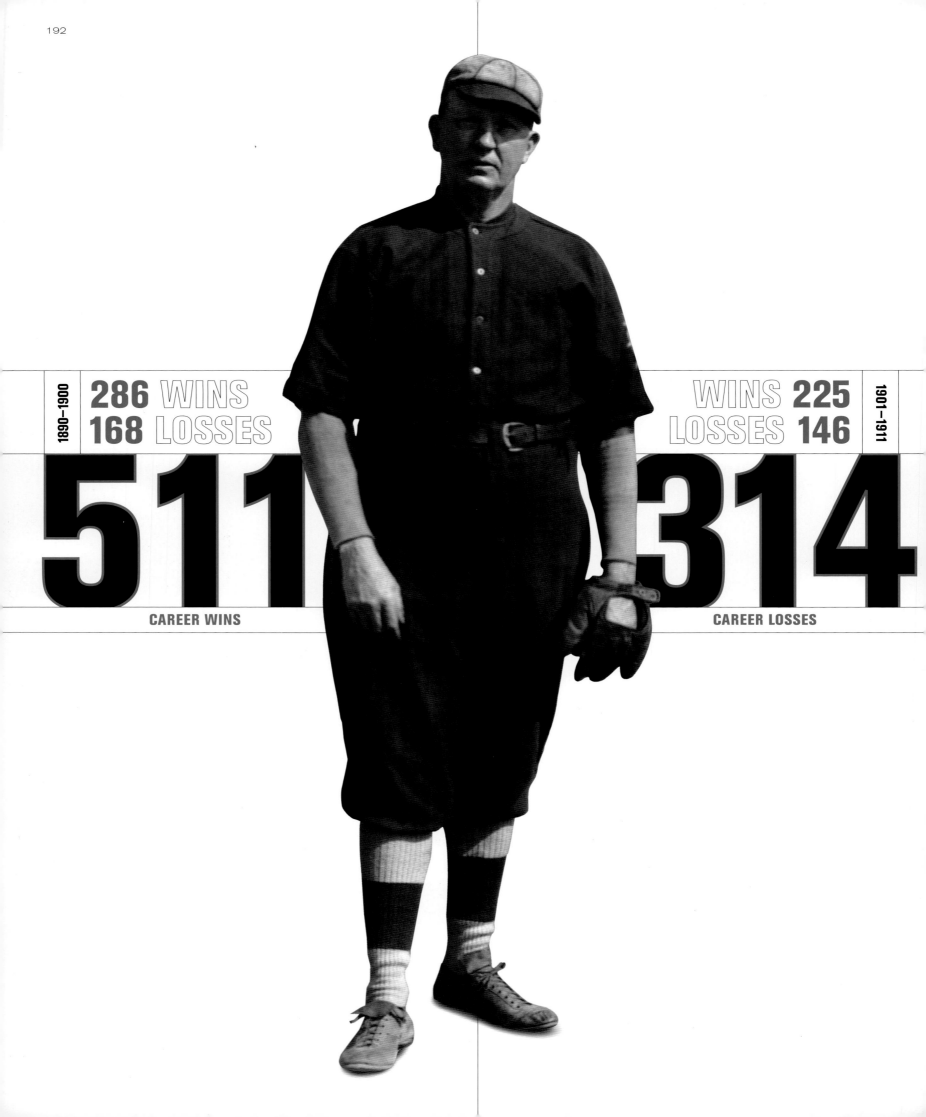

1890–1900

286 WINS
168 LOSSES

WINS **225**
LOSSES **146**

1901–1911

511

314

CAREER WINS

CAREER LOSSES

t's even more illuminating to split Young's career along lines that pay more attention to the evolution of baseball rules than to the calendar. The pitcher's current position of 60 feet, 6 inches from home plate, was set in 1893. From then through 1902 — a logical demarcation to be explained shortly — Young led the majors with 278 victories. In fact, only five other pitchers had even half as many victories as Young during that time: Kid Nichols, 237; Clark Griffith, 194; Pink Hawley, 162; Brickyard Kennedy, 162; and Ted Breitenstein, 150.

In 1903, the American League adopted the current rule charging strikes for foul balls, except for third strike. (The National League had implemented the rule two years earlier.)

From 1903 until 1909 — his last good season, at the age of 42 — Young won another 146 games. For those seven seasons, his total was topped only by a pair of Hall of Famers: Christy Mathewson (202) and Eddie Plank (149).

It's not at all a stretch to say Young had a pair of Hall of Fame careers back-to-back. This time, we'll split his career down the middle, with 11 seasons in each half. From 1890 through 1900, Young posted a record of 286-168 with a 3.04 ERA. If the ERA is higher than expected, keep in mind that the 1890s was a hitters' decade, with the mound moved back 10 feet to its current distance, and no strikes charged for foul balls. Only two pitchers in major league history came within 25 victories, 25 losses and 25 ERA points of Young's totals for that period. Both are Hall of Famers: Bob Feller (266-162, 3.25) and Jim Palmer (268-152, 2.86).

For the second half of his career, Young was 225-146 with a 2.12 ERA. No pitchers can be found that close to Young in all three categories. So we'll use different points of comparison. During the period from 1900 to 1919--the last 20 years of the dead-ball era, played almost entirely under the modern foul-ball rules — the only pitchers with as many victories and as low an ERA as Young were Walter Johnson (297-191, 1.64) and Christy Mathewson (373-185, 2.11), the only pitchers who were "charter members" of the Hall of Fame.

Durability was certainly one of Young's greatest attributes. Even during the 10-year period during which Young pitched at the new, longer distance but before foul balls were charged as strikes, he still averaged 42 starts per season and completed 93 percent of them. Young's record of 511 career victories may never be broken, but it's more likely to fall than his mark of 750 complete games. To place that in context: As the 1900s draw to a close, current veteran pitchers such as Kevin Brown, David Cone and John Smoltz haven't made even half as many starts as Young completed. Only one active pitcher has even 100 complete games (Roger Clemens).

Young was so prolific over such a long career that he held the record for appearances by a pitcher until 1968, when Hoyt Wilhelm surpassed his totals. Somewhere in the fine print, it should be noted Young pitched an average of 8.1 innings per game during his career and Wilhelm an average of 2.1 innings.

Just as impressive as Young's durability was his control. He had the major leagues' lowest rate of walks per nine innings 12 times over a period of 14 seasons from 1893 to 1906. No other pitcher led the majors even half as often; Christy Mathewson ranks second, having led five times. Young also led his league in strikeouts twice. Most fans know that Nolan Ryan broke Walter Johnson's longstanding record for career strikeouts. Few are aware that Johnson took the baton from Cy Young.

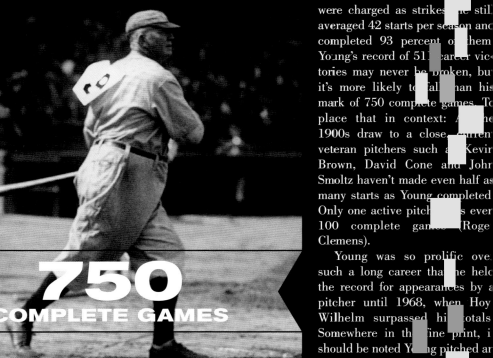

750
COMPLETE GAMES

THE CY YOUNG AWARD WAS INSTITUTED IN 1956. THE FACT IT CARRIES HIS
NAME PROBABLY OWES MORE TO THE FACT YOUNG HAD DIED IN LATE 1955 THAN
IT DOES A PREFERENCE OVER JOHNSON OR MATHEWSON, WHO PRECEDED
HIM INTO THE HALL OF FAME. IT WAS ORIGINALLY CALLED THE CY YOUNG
MEMORIAL AWARD, BUT IT HAS SERVED TO KEEP ALIVE THE MEMORY OF
A PITCHER WHOSE ACCOMPLISHMENTS FAR EXCEEDED THOSE OF MOST OF THE
PITCHERS WHO WERE HONORED WITH THE AWARD THE BEARS HIS NAME.

CHRISTY MATHE

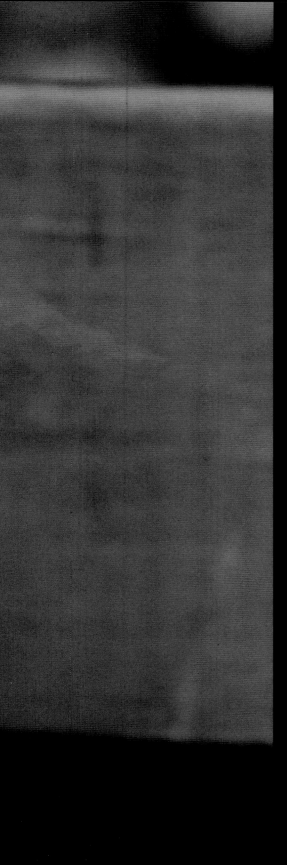

HE LED THE NATIONAL LEAGUE IN WINS FOUR TIMES AND IN STRIKEOUTS FIVE TIMES. DURING A FOUR-YEAR PERIOD FROM 1904 TO 1907, THERE WERE FIVE OTHER HALL OF FAME PITCHERS ACTIVE WHO DEBUTED WITHIN TWO YEARS OF MATHEWSON, WHOSE 110-45 RECORD DURING THAT TIME WAS BY FAR THE BEST OF THEM. THE OTHERS: JACK CHESBRO (93-54), ADDIE JOSS (82-42), JOE MCGINNITY (101-53), EDDIE PLANK (93-51), AND VIC WILLIS (74-78).

Christy Mathewson was the best pitcher of the first decade of the century. Mathewson also was a contemporary of Cy Young, whose career began 10 years earlier than Mathewson's but spanned 22 years. From Mathewson's rookie season of 1901 through 1909, Young's last good season, they were the two winningest pitchers in the majors. But Mathewson's 236-109 record and his 1.94 ERA were better than Young's figures (211-127, 2.02). Although Mathewson and Young pitched in different leagues, the leaguewide ERAs were nearly identical during those years: 2.78 in the NL, 2.81 in the AL.

In a couple ways, Mathewson's accomplishments are reminiscent of Bob Gibson's. He was a dominant National League strikeout pitcher with several ERAs comparable to Gibson's 1.12 in 1968, and he had extraordinary success in the World Series.

Earned runs weren't tallied and recorded on an official basis until 1912. But according to the commonly accepted figures for years prior to that, Mathewson was a five-time ERA leader. Dead-ball era or not, contemporary fans can't help but be reminded of Gibson's great 1968 season when seeing Mathewson's best marks: 1.27 in 1905 and 1.15 in 1909. And for the record, the National League ERA in 1905 was 2.99, the same as it was in 1968. (The NL mark in 1909 was 2.59.)

Like Gibson 60 years later, Mathewson was at his best in World Series play. In 1905, the National League was fighting for its reputation against the upstart American League — in only its fifth season of play, but already having signed away some of the NL's best players — among them, Nap Lajoie, Willie Keeler, Jesse Burkett and Cy Young (all future Hall of Famers). Mathewson's manager John McGraw was also involved in a personal feud with AL President Ban Johnson. With that as a backdrop, Mathewson made three World Series starts over six days, and he pitched three complete-game shutouts. His Giants defeated Connie Mack's A's in five games.

Mathewson pitched in three other World Series, in consecutive seasons from 1911 to 1913, seemingly without distinction. He started a total of eight games with a 2-5 record. However, he lost twice to the Red Sox in 1912, with both losses fueled by unearned runs. For 11 World Series starts, Mathewson's ERA was 1.15.

PLAYER	BORN	BIRTHPLACE	BATS	THROWS	HEIGHT	WEIGHT	MAJOR LEAGUE DEBUT
CHRISTY MATHEWSON	08/12/1880	FACTORYVILLE, PA	R	R	6'1.5"	195	07/17/00

...his achievements, nothing written about Mathewson ...would be complete without discussing his character. He was a true hero, idolized by his fans and respected by his teammates and opponents, not only for his ability but for who he was. Even his manager, the rough John McGraw, made concessions to Matty's character.

For example, many reference sources cite his reluctance to pitch on Sundays, and McGraw's accommodation of his wishes. The fact is, Mathewson never started a game on Sunday in his entire major league career.

If Hank Aaron never had played on Sunday, he would have hit only 607 home runs. If Cal Ripken never had played on Sunday, ...his longest playing streak would have been 12 games. But Mathewson managed a great career despite having to adjust his pitching schedule according to his principles. The interesting thing is that when he pitched on a Saturday on short rest (i.e., with two days between starts) or on a Monday on long rest (four days), his career record was 30-14 (682) — higher than his .656 winning percentage in other starts.

Times were different then. At the turn of the century, many teams didn't schedule Sunday games. In general, the teams in the midwest did, the east coast teams did not. There were no Sunday games in Cleveland until 1911; none in Washington D.C. until 1918; none in New York until 1919. Boston held out until 1923 and Philadelphia until 1934. But for Mathewson never have started on a Sunday, on nothing more than principle, is truly astounding to fans of today.

Mathewson was the kind of hero who was popular in kids' fiction books in a simpler time. He was handsome and athletic, but also intelligent and principled. He was a class president a Bucknell, where he headed two literary societies and sang in the glee club. He was without the kind of attitude we often see in superstars of today. Matty even died young, at the age of 45, o injuries sustained in a war time accident involving mustard gas He was given a funeral befitting a beloved and genuine hero. In closing, we'll quote Ring Lardner's poetic epitaph:

"MY EYES ARE EVER MISTY AS I PEN THESE LINES TO CHRISTY;

MY HEART IS FULL OF HEAVINESS TODAY. MAY THE

FLOWERS NE'ER WITHER, MATTY ON YOUR GRAVE IN CINCINNATI

WHICH YOU'VE CHOSEN FOR YOUR FINAL FADEAWAY."

11 WORLD SERIES STARTS

1.15 ERA

WARREN SPAHN IS BEST KNOWN AS THE WINNINGEST LEFT-HANDER IN MAJOR LEAGUE HISTORY — AN UNUSUAL ACCOMPLISHMENT FOR A PITCHER WHO DIDN'T EARN HIS FIRST VICTORY UNTIL AFTER WORLD WAR II. ALTHOUGH HE PITCHED DECADES AFTER THE INTRODUCTION OF THE LIVE BALL, SPAHN HAD A CAREER THAT SEEMS TO HAVE BEEN PULLED FROM THE ANNALS OF THE DEAD-BALL ERA. FOR A BATTER, THAT WOULD MEAN A DEMOTION TO THE DOUBLE-A LEVEL. FOR A PITCHER, IT'S THE HIGHEST COMPLIMENT AND WORTH A TRIP TO COOPERSTOWN.

PLAYER	BORN	BIRTHPLACE	BATS	THROWS	HEIGHT	WEIGHT	MAJOR LEAGUE DEBUT
WARREN SPAHN	04/23/21	BUFFALO, NY	L	L	6'	175	04/19/42

SPAHN'S TOTAL OF 363 CAREER VICTORIES WOULD HAVE BEEN THE THIRD HIGHEST EVEN DURING THE DEAD-BALL ERA. ON A LIST OF VICTORIES DURING THE LIVE-BALL ERA, IT STANDS HEAD-AND-SHOULDERS ABOVE THE REST.

Pitchers compiled much higher victory totals before 1920 (both within a single season and over the course of a career). From that point on, the livelier ball forced them to bear down on every batter. During the dead-ball era, home runs were infrequent and teams normally needed a rally to score. Accordingly, pitchers often coasted, bearing down selectively, usually with runners on base and a scoring threat in progress. This allowed pitchers to throw fewer pitches in general, throw their best stuff at top speed only when necessary, pitch deeper into games, and make more starts in a season.

Using a "dead" ball, pitchers earned decisions in 91 percent of their starts; using the live ball, the percentage is 76 percent. Admittedly, the percentages have varied even within those periods of time and they have been affected by other changes of rules and fashion, but by nothing as much as the change to the ball in 1920. As a result, there were as many pitchers with 300 victories during the 44 years of the dead-ball era (covering 651 "team-seasons") as there were during the 80 seasons to date using the live ball (1,622 team-seasons, more than half of them using a longer 162-game schedule than existed in the dead-ball days).

WINNINGEST PITCHERS SINCE 1920

TOMMY JOHN *288*	EARLY WYNN *300*	LEFTY GROVE *300*	TOM SEAVER *311*	GAYLORD PERRY *314*
PHIL NIEKRO *318*	DON SUTTON *324*		NOLAN RYAN *324*	STEVE CARLTON *329*

Spahn himself earned a decision in 88 percent of his starts, another statistic more characteristic of the dead-ball era. Over the 20 seasons from 1946 to 1965, only one pitcher had a higher average: Bob Lemon (90 percent). To some degree, Spahn's (and Lemon's) high percentage reflected the fact that he hit well enough not to require a pinch-hitter in some situations that would have prompted the removal of other pitchers. His career home-run rate of one per 53.5 at-bats is nearly identical to those of Billy Martin and Bill Buckner. (The only players to hit home runs in more than 15 consecutive seasons for the Braves are Hank Aaron and Spahn — not the more obvious candidate, Eddie Mathews.)

Spahn's total of 363 career victories would have been the third highest even during the dead-ball era. On a list of victories during the live-ball era, it stands head-and-shoulders above the rest. The chart above lists the winningest pitchers since 1920. Note that the gap of 34 victories between Spahn and the runner-up is greater than the number of victories spanning the next eight pitchers.

Any time a category leader stands so far above the pack it is an impressive feat. In Spahn's case, it's even more so because he didn't win his first major league game until he was 25 years old. Spahn is not unique in that regard among 300-game winners. Eddie Plank and Lefty Grove didn't earn their first victories until age 25; Phil Niekro and Old Hoss Radbourn did so at age 26. Then again, it's Spahn who ranks fifth all-time in career victories — a dominating first during the live-ball era — and who won at least 34 games more than any of them.

Moreover, it wasn't as though Spahn spent his early 20s gaining experience in the minors. In 1941, at the age of 20, he led the Three-I

League (a Class-B league operating in Iowa, Illinois and Indiana) in victories and ERA. A year later, he started the season with the Braves, then won 17 games with a 1.96 ERA after being sent to Hartford in the Eastern League, which earned him a September recall to the majors.

But like so many established major leaguers of the era, Spahn was called into military service. His missed three full seasons and part of another as well; he wasn't released by the Army until June 1946. He joined the Braves in July, went 8-5 after the All-Star break, then led the league in ERA in 1947, his first full season in the majors.

That was also the first of Spahn's 13 20-win seasons. No other pitcher had more than eight 20-win seasons during the live-ball era; in fact, Spahn's total is one more than the combined total of the four other winningest pitchers of that era: Steve Carlton (6), Nolan Ryan (2), Don Sutton (1) and Phil Niekro (3). Spahn's total was matched only by two Hall of Fame pitchers from the turn of the century: Cy Young (16) and Christy Mathewson (13).

The span of 16 seasons between Spahn's first and last 20-win seasons is one short of Young's all-time record and four years more than anyone else in the live-ball era. (Bob Feller, Gaylord Perry and Roger Clemens spanned 12 years.)

Spahn was a winning machine, who compiled by far the highest victory total in the live-ball era, despite having his career delayed three years or more. He maintained his peak at a later age than any other pitcher in history; he was the oldest pitcher ever to win 20 games in a season (23 victories at age 42 in 1963). His career was typical of what pitchers of a half-century earlier were capable of, and only because they worked in a less taxing environment.

363

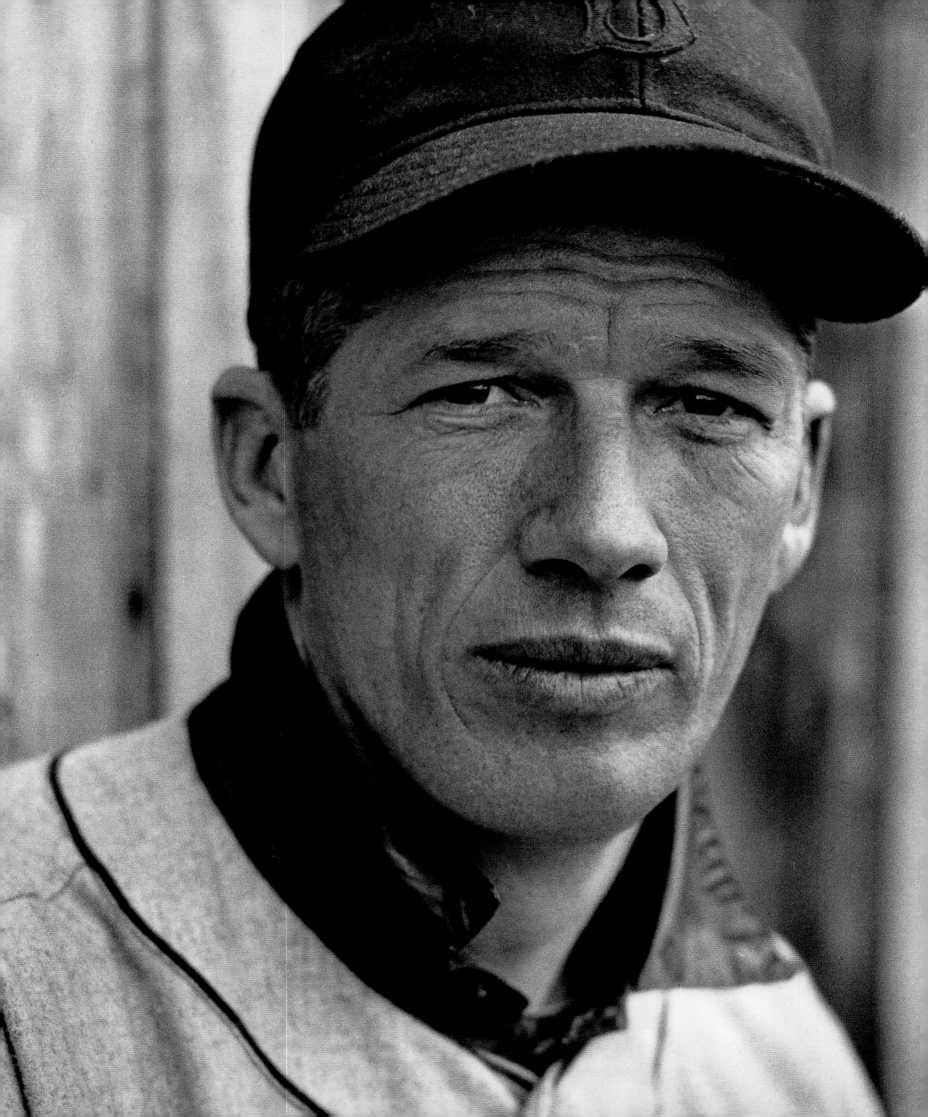

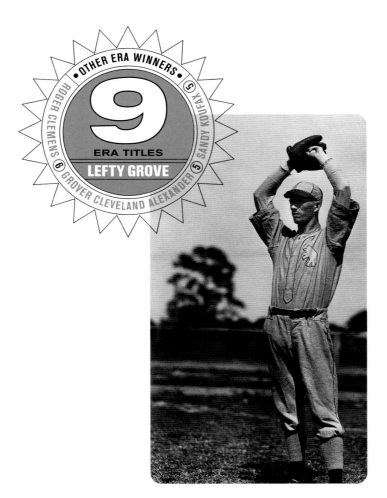

OTHER ERA WINNERS

9

ERA TITLES

LEFTY GROVE

ROGER CLEMENS ⑥ GROVER CLEVELAND ALEXANDER ⑤ SANDY KOUFAX ⑤

LEFTY GROVE

WHETHER LEFTY GROVE WAS THE GREATEST PITCHER IN MAJOR LEAGUE HISTORY IS DEBATABLE. CERTAINLY CASES COULD BE MADE, AND HAVE BEEN MADE IN THIS BOOK, FOR SEVERAL OTHERS. BUT THERE IS LITTLE DOUBT THAT ANY PITCHER DOMINATED HIS ERA TO THE EXTENT THAT GROVE DID.

PLAYER	BORN	BIRTHPLACE	BATS	THROWS	HEIGHT	WEIGHT	MAJOR LEAGUE DEBUT
LEFTY GROVE	03/06/1900	LONACONING, MD	L	L	6'3"	190	04/14/25

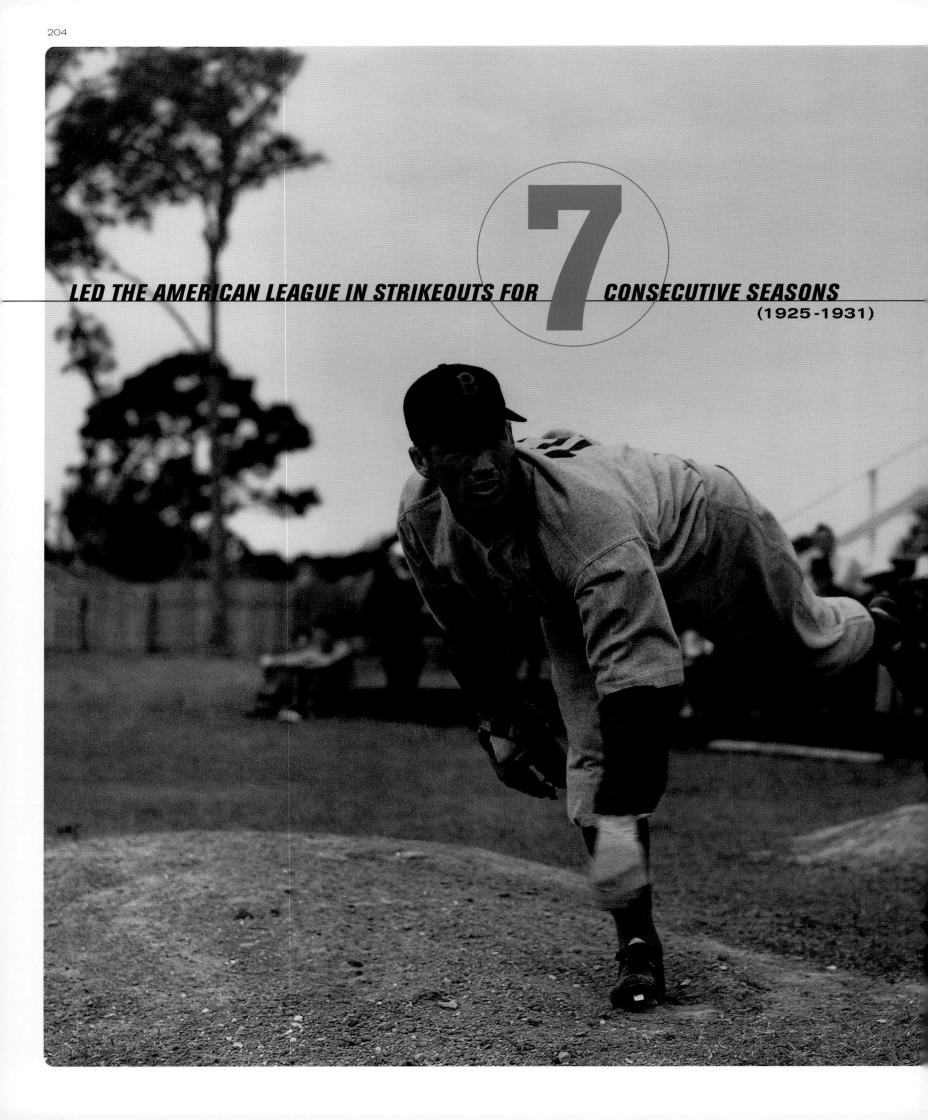

LED THE AMERICAN LEAGUE IN STRIKEOUTS FOR **7** *CONSECUTIVE SEASONS*
(1925-1931)

STRIKE OUTS

TOTALS FROM 1913-1962

BOB FELLER	★ 2,581 ★
WARREN SPAHN	★ 2,313 ★
EARLY WYNN	★ 2,305 ★
WALTER JOHNSON	★ 2,291 ★
LEFTY GROVE	★ 2,266 ★

Grove won nine ERA titles, three more than any other pitcher in major league history and more than twice as many as any pitcher other than Roger Clemens (6), Grover Cleveland Alexander (5) and Sandy Koufax (5). Grove did so despite splitting his career between teams that played in hitters' parks — the A's at Shibe Park and the Red Sox at Fenway Park. He has the highest winning percentage among 300-game winners (.680) and he ranks third all-time among pitchers with at least 150 victories, behind only Bob Caruthers (.692) and Whitey Ford (.690).

At his peak, Grove was as close to unbeatable as any pitcher who ever played the game. The A's won three consecutive American League titles from 1929 to 1931 and Grove posted a record of 79-15 in those three seasons. Looking a little more closely, from July 1928 through July 1931, Grove had an incredible 85-15 mark, by far the most victories in this century over a span of 100 decisions. Only two other pitchers reached the 80-mark: Sandy Koufax (81) and Mordecai Brown (80).

Like Koufax, Grove spent the first few years of his career trying to master his control. As a result, he didn't win his first major league game until age 25. (Only three 300-game winners earned their first victories at a more advanced age: Old Hoss Radbourn, Phil Niekro and Eddie Plank.) Grove led the majors in walks as a rookie in 1925. But manager Connie Mack is said to have counseled Grove to take more time between pitches.

He made a breakthrough in his third season, walking an average of 2.7 batters per nine innings compared to 6.0 in 1925 and producing the first of seven consecutive 20-win seasons, the longest streak of the live-ball era. During those seven years, he led the AL in victories four times, ranked second once and third twice.

GROVE'S 3.06 CAREER ERA DOES NOT APPEAR REMARKABLE, ESPECIALLY IN THE COMPANY OF PITCHERS FROM THE DEAD-BALL ERA OR THOSE WHO PLAYED IN THE LOWER-SCORING 1960S AND 1970S. THE FACT IS, GROVE PITCHED IN THE HIGHEST-SCORING ERA IN MAJOR LEAGUE HISTORY.

The American League ERA during Grove's career (with each season weighted in proportion to the number of innings Grove pitched) was 4.41.

Grove was also one of baseball's most under appreciated strikeout artists. He led the American League in strikeouts in seven consecutive seasons (1925-1931), an impressive feat on its own. The only other pitchers to lead a league seven straight years are Walter Johnson (12), Nolan Ryan (9), Dazzy Vance (7) and Bob Feller (7). But Grove added an exclamation point because he led the league in each of his first seven seasons (as did Vance).

Again, Grove's totals are more than they appear on account of the era in which he pitched. He struck out 200 batters in a season just once; but from 1917 to 1937, that was the only 200-strikeout season in the American League. Even higher totals were non-existent: From 1900 to 1912, there were four 300-stikeout seasons; from 1963 to 1999, there were 24. But during the 50 years in between, from 1913 through 1962, there was only one season of 300 strikeouts — by Bob Feller in 1946 (348). During that half-century of low strikeout totals, Grove ranked fifth with a total of 2,266 stikeouts, behind Feller (2,581), Warren Spahn (2,313), Early Wynn (2,305), and Walter Johnson (2,291). None of those totals looks imposing compared to the best totals of all-time; 18 pitchers have higher career totals. But all of those pitchers were strikeout aces by the standards of the time.

★

BRETT, GEORGE [1973–1993]
MATHEWS, EDDIE [1952–1968]
MOLITOR, PAUL [1978–1998]
ROBINSON, BROOKS [1955–1977]
SCHMIDT, MIKE [1972–1989]
TRAYNOR, PIE [1920–1937]

★

THIRD
BASE

NO MEMBER OF THE ALL–CENTURY TEAM HAS MORE VALUE
HIDDEN BEHIND HIS BASIC STATISTICAL RECORD THAN BROOKS
ROBINSON. IT'S A TESTAMENT TO ROBINSON'S DESERVED REPUTATION
FOR CLUTCH HITTING AND INCOMPARABLE FIELDING THAT
AT THE TIME OF HIS RETIREMENT, HE WAS WIDELY CONSIDERED

BROOKS ROBINSON

THE GREATEST THIRD BASEMAN IN MAJOR LEAGUE HISTORY.

hat's not to say Robinson lacks the basic trappings of the all-time greats. He was the American League's Most Valuable Player in 1964 when he led the league in RBIs and ranked second in batting average despite a third-place finish by his Orioles team. He finished third in the MVP voting in 1965, and second in 1966. He even finished a very close third to Roger Maris and Mickey Mantle in 1960, when he batted .294 with 14 homers when voters seemed first to recognize the value of his glove.

16 CONSECUTIVE GOLD GLOVES

But there are three areas in which a quick look at the kinds of statistics that appear on bubble gum cards greatly understate Robinson's value. First, they provide no context for his .267 career batting average, compiled in a pitcher's park during a pitcher's era. Second, they do not highlight his clutch hitting and disproportionately high RBI totals. Third, they do not properly recognize his standing as the greatest fielding third baseman of all time.

Robinson's career batting average is modest for any starting major leaguer today, let alone the players on the All–Century Team. But of all the Hall of Famers, only two played during a span of years in which their league's average was lower than the .249 mark during Robinson's career. (They are Luis Aparicio and Harmon Killebrew, both at .248, both contemporaries) Robinson's average was 8 percent higher than the league mark — comparable to Hack Wilson, who parlayed the same margin during a hitters' era into a .307 career mark.

PLAYER	BORN	BIRTHPLACE	BATS	THROWS	HEIGHT	WEIGHT	MAJOR LEAGUE DEBUT
BROOKS ROBINSON	05/18/37	LITTLEROCK, AR	R	R	6'1"	190	09/17/55

ROBINSON DROVE IN MORE RUNS THAN HIS BASIC STATISTICS SUGGEST HE SHOULD HAVE. THAT IN ITSELF IS A LEGITIMATE DEFINITION OF CLUTCH HITTING. AND BECAUSE THIS WAS A CAREER-LONG PATTERN, IT'S LIKELY ROBINSON HIT MUCH BETTER WITH RUNNERS IN SCORING POSITION THAN HE DID AT OTHER TIMES.

Robinson played his home games at Memorial Stadium, another negative influence on his batting average. That ballpark suppressed batting averages by approximately 4 percent (a figure derived by comparing batting averages there to those in Orioles road games) — equal to about 10 batting-average points. Among contemporary stadiums, only Oakland Coliseum and the Astrodome had a greater negative effect.

Robinson was considered one of the best clutch hitters of his generation. One of the things we've learned in the past quarter-century, during which various measures of clutch hitting have been recorded, is that reputations don't always survive the facts. That doesn't appear to be the case with Robinson, who unfortunately pre-dates the era in which one simply could check his batting average with runners in scoring position or in the late innings of close games.

But one thing appears certain: Robinson drove in more runs than his basic statistics suggest he should have. That in itself is a legitimate definition of clutch hitting. And because this was a career-long pattern, it's likely Robinson hit much better with runners in scoring position than he did at other times.

★ .267 BA ★ 8% HIGHER THAN LEAGUE ★

Through a mathematical regression, we were able to use at-bats, home runs and batting averages to estimate the number of runs a player should have driven in. We ran these projections for the 42 players who had at least 4,000 at-bats in the American League during the uninterrupted span of Robinson's career as a regular starter (1960 to 1975). During that time, Robinson drove in 148 more runs than expected (1,270 to 1,112), by far the highest margin among those 42 players. Only two other players were plus-100 or better: Boog Powell (+110) and Sal Bando (+103).

Finally, there is the issue of Robinson's fielding. He won 16 consecutive Gold Glove awards — the last of them at the age of 38 (more on that shortly) — at a position requiring extraordinary reflexes. He led the league in assists eight times, a record. But what's truly amazing is that his career fielding percentage of .971 remains the highest in major league history.

The records for second basemen and shortstops are both held by contemporary players — Ryne Sandberg and Omar Vizquel, respectively. With the advent of artificial turf, which substantially reduces errors by second basemen, third basemen and shortstops, it's to be expected that infielders of the past 25 years would have surpassed the marks of players from previous eras. It doesn't mean they were better fielders than players of the past; it means they had better equipment (both on their hands and under their feet). But the last player even to approach Robinson's record was Steve Buechele, and it wasn't that close. He would have needed to handle 345 more chances without an error to pass Brooks. The record for consecutive errorless chances at third base is 261, by Don Money, and the best career rate, Robinson's, is one error every 35 chances.

A telling indication of Robinson's fielding ability is the fact that in 1975, at the age of 38, he played 143 games at third base for the Orioles (and he led all third basemen in fielding) despite batting .201 with just six homers and no stolen bases. Only one other player in the live-ball era had as many at-bats in a season as Robinson did in 1975 and produced batting, slugging and on-base averages as low. (The player was Jim Levey, who posted the second-highest fielding percentage among AL shortstops that season playing for the St. Louis Browns, but never again played in the majors.)

Consider what that meant: The Orioles, running second in the AL East for the second half of the season — and narrowing the Red Sox lead throughout September — determined that it was worth starting the league's most unproductive hitter in more than 40 years on virtually an everyday basis. The reason was his glove. (Incidentally, that also illustrates how Robinson's great fielding was yet another negative influence on his career batting average. A lesser fielding player never would have been given those 747 at-bats over Robinson's final three seasons, during which he hit .201, dropping his career mark from .272 to .267.)

If he was good enough at 38 to compensate for low productivity that would have kept others on the bench (or driven them to retirement), younger fans can only imagine how great he was in his prime.

Mike Schmidt is one of only eight players to have won three MVP awards and he did it primarily by hitting home runs. Schmidt won eight home run titles over 13 years from 1974 to 1986, perfectly positioned as a bridge between Hank Aaron and Mark McGwire, baseball's career and single-season home run kings. Aaron surpassed Babe Ruth's total of 714 homers in April 1974. Mark McGwire made his auspicious debut with 49 homers as a rookie in 1987. In the interim, Mike Schmidt was baseball's dominant home run threat.

Other than Babe Ruth, no one led his league in home runs more often than Schmidt. Ruth led the American League 12 times; Schmidt led the NL a record eight times (one more than Ralph Kiner). From 1974 through 1986, Schmidt filled the Aaron-McGwire gap by hitting nearly 100 more homers than anyone else in the majors. The top five: Schmidt, 476; Dave Kingman, 383; Reggie Jackson, 359, Jim Rice, 351, and George Foster, 328. (Schmidt shares a similar record with Hank Aaron and Rogers Hornsby. They are the only players to lead the National League in RBIs four times.)

Unlike other members of the "500-Home Run Club", Schmid didn't post perennially high batting averages. Babe Ruth batted .300 or better 16 times, Hank Aaron 13 times, Willie Mays 10 times, and Frank Robinson nine times. Schmidt did so only once — a .316 mark in 1981 — when a players' strike compromised what might have been the greatest season in his Hall of Fame career.

But Schmidt's unremarkable batting average — he batted .267 for his career — vastly understated his ability to reach base. He led the NL in walks four times, including in 1981 when he also led the league in RBIs. That's a rare and impressive parlay. The only other player to lead his league in both walks and

PLAYER	BORN	BIRTHPLACE	BATS	THROWS	HEIGHT	WEIGHT	MAJOR LEAGUE DEBUT
MIKE SCHMIDT	09/27/49	DAYTON, OH	R	R	6'2"	203	09/12/72

RBIs in the last 25 years of the century was Will Clark (1988). Although Schmidt ranked in the NL's top 10 in batting average only twice, he did so in on-base average 11 times, leading the league three consecutive seasons from 1981 to 1983.

Just as Schmidt's home-run totals put him in company with the greatest power hitters ever, his fielding statistics placed him among the best of the best at the hot corner. He won 10 Gold Gloves, a total attained by only eight other players. He led NL third basemen in assists seven times and in double plays six times. The only player to win more assist titles was Brooks Robinson, who led the AL eight times. No third basemen led his league in double plays more than Schmidt did (though Heinie Groh and Ron Santo also led the NL six times).

As both the greatest home run hitter of the era between Aaron and McGwire, and the best fielder at his position in the post-Brooks Robinson era, Schmidt fulfilled the evolving requirements of the third base position better than anyone before or after.

NUMBER OF GOLD GLOVES
10

LED THE LEAGUE IN ASSISTS
7
TIMES

LED THE LEAGUE IN DOUBLE PLAYS
6
TIMES

12
HOME RUN TITLES
BABE RUTH

8
HOME RUN TITLES
MIKE SCHMIDT

7
HOME RUN TITLES
RALPH KINER

SCHMIDT LED THE NL IN WALKS FOUR TIMES, INCLUDING IN 1981 WHEN HE ALSO LED THE LEAGUE IN RBIs. THAT'S A RARE AND IMPRESSIVE PARLAY. THE ONLY OTHER PLAYER TO LEAD HIS LEAGUE IN BOTH WALKS AND RBIs IN THE LAST 25 YEARS WAS WILL CLARK (1988).

"A GAME OF GREAT CHARM IN THE ADOPTION OF MATHEMATICAL
MEASUREMENTS TO THE TIMING OF HUMAN MOVEMENTS, THE
EXACTITUDE AND ADJUSTMENTS OF PHYSICAL ABILITY TO
HAZARDOUS CHANCE. THE SPEED OF THE LEGS, THE DEXTERITY OF
THE BODY, THE GRACE OF THE SWING, THE ELUSIVENESS OF THE
SLIDE — THESE ARE THE FEATURES THAT MAKE AMERICANS
EVERYWHERE FORGET THE LAST SYLLABLE OF A MAN'S LAST NAME
OR THE PIGMENTATION OF HIS SKIN."

★

BRANCH RICKEY
MAY 1960 BEFORE A CONGRESSIONAL COMMITTEE

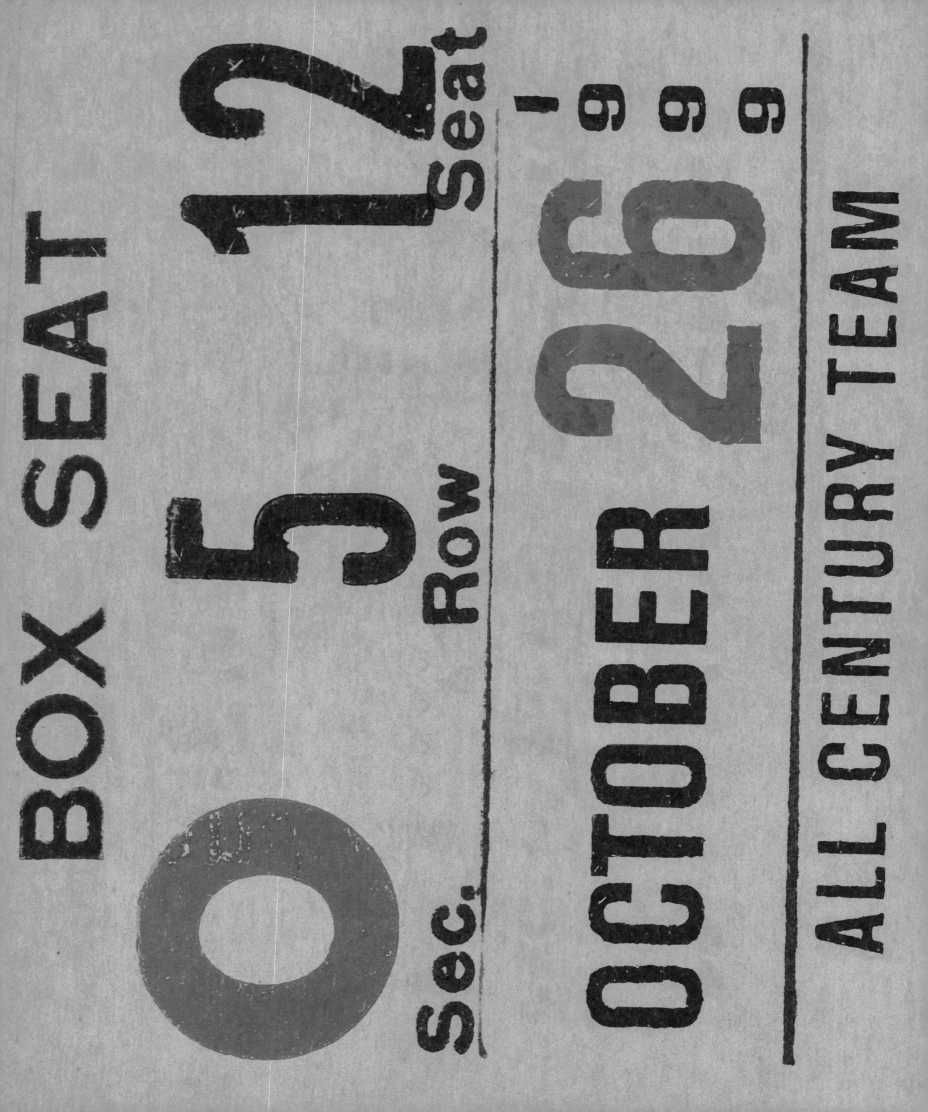